the
mexican
**Revolution**

3

# the mexican Revolution

a historic politico-military compendium

Luis M. Garfias

 PANORAMA EDITORIAL, S.A.

Drawings by:
  José Narro

First edition in english: 1979
Fourth reprint: 1990
© Panorama Editorial, S.A.
  Leibnitz 31, Col. Anzures
  11590 México, D.F.

PANORAMA SERIES
  Under the direction of:
  Federico Santiago E.

Translated by:
  Ana María Jolly de Espinosa

Photographs by:
  Centro Regional Hidalgo I.N.A.H.

Printed in Mexico
Impreso en México
ISBN 968-38-0028-9

# Index

# 1

Immediate political, socio-economic and military events leading to the 1910 Revolution against the Porfirio Díaz regime. Liberal background. Díaz-Creelman interview and its consequences. *The Presidential Succession* of Francisco I. Madero. The political struggle of 1910.

The outlook in Mexico City at the end of 1910 could not have been more optimistic. The Centennial of the Independence had just been celebrated with great splendor: countries having relations with Mexico sent plenipotentiary ambassadors and ministers; very distinguished people came, among which were the personal representative of Alfonso XIII, King of Spain, Marquis Camilo de Polavieja, who brought with him the uniform of Generalissimo Morelos to deliver to the Mexican Government; Mr. Curtiss Guild, special ambassador of the United States of America; also attending were Mr. Carl Buenz, special ambassador of Germany, Mr. Chan Tin Fang, the Chinese Ambassador; Major General Enrique Loynaz of Cuba; Mr. Paul Lefebre of France, and many other dignitaries who helped make the Centennial unusually brilliant. Well advanced in years General Diaz was at the height of his glory. Mexico was a country respected by the great powers, its credit was good, and, in general terms, prosperity and peace were apparent.

Inaugurations and monuments to foreign personalities were spectacles frequently seen in those days. His excellency the Minister of France, Paul Lefebre, accompanied by Admiral De Castries, was present at the ceremony in which the first stone was placed for a statue in honor of the learned chemist Pasteur, which was given to Mexico by the French colony residing in Mexico City. The American colony did something similar by presenting to Mexico a statue of George Washington; the ceremony was presided over by President Díaz in the company of Ambassadors Guild and Wilson.

German Ambassador Buenz solemnly inaugurated a monument to Humboldt, and thus it was believed that Mexico marched along the path of progress. However, behind all this a very different reality was being lived. The Mexican people, the real people who lived removed from the false glitter, were already tired of those long years which, even if they had brought peace, were at a cost of great social injustice. The prolonged tenure of Díaz had tired the country which desired a real democracy.

The gravest problem was agrarian. Most of the farmers were not landowners; there were enormous latifundia in the possession of a few families. In the year 1910, in which the total population of Mexico was 15,160,269 inhabitants, there were 830 landholders in the Republic, 410,345 farmers and 3,123,975 day laborers working in 8,431 haciendas and 48,433 ranches. This indicates that 80% of the population depended on rural wages, which were from 18 to 25 cents per day. Their wages scarcely provided a meager meal since the daily diet consisted of tortillas, chili, beans, and pulque (a drink obtained from the fermented juice of the maguey plant). Prices for staple foods were 13 cents a kilo for rice and ten cents for beans. The peons worked at enormous haciendas where the owners were never to be found, as they divided their time and leisure between Mexico City and Europe. The great majority of these unprotected farmers lived in humble houses made of adobe, lacking the most basic sanitary conditions; their household furnishings were quite primitive and a wife and numerous offspring served to complete the picture. In the haciendas were found the well-known "tiendas de raya" (payroll shops), in which, under a credit system, the farmers were paid their wages with merchandise: beans, corn, soap, blankets and "aguardiente". Because of the high prices and the miserable wages, the farmer was normally in debt for life. To this was added the system of working the land which was not modern as the owners did not make an effort to introduce new methods; this in turn exhausted the soil. The economic crisis became evident in 1910 when corn in the amount of 27 million pesos had to be imported, in addition to spending 94 million on other grains.

At the beginning of the century, the exploitation of petroleum had been initiated in Mexico by granting concessions to foreigners for its exploitation. Standard Oil, "El Aguila" and Royal Dutch Shell were among the important companies established in the country. Foreign investors under the protection of General Díaz began to create industries and exploit raw materials. The result of this was the necessity to create a vast railroad system. Mining, which for centuries had been controlled by Spaniards and some Mexicans, also underwent important changes with the help of foreign capital; the textile industry, which was controlled by Spaniards, was modernized and the cultivation of cotton increased. In 1910 there were 146 factories which produced $43,370,012 pesos and employed 32,229 workers.

This resulted in an apparent financial bonanza during the first decade of the century. The government turned a deaf ear to the public clamor and was unaware that it was giving birth to a revolution which would bring great social changes. The labor movement, aware of its situation, began to agitate in 1906. The ideologists Lázaro Gutiérrez de Lara, Sarabia, Ricardo Flores Magón and others, by means of the newspaper *Regeneración* demanded rights for the working class. During that year two strikes occurred in Mexico which were brutally repressed. The first took place in Cananea, Sonora when the miners, disgusted with the annoying conditions in which they lived, called a strike to improve their living conditions. The second strike occurred seven months later in the great textile center in Río Blanco, Veracruz. Both strikes were declared null and void by the military. The leaders of the first strike, Manuel M. Diéguez and Esteban Baca Calderón, were imprisoned, while in the second, Rafael Moreno and Manuel Juárez, President and Secretary of the "Círculo de Obreros Libres" (Organization of Free Workers) were shot against the wall of the payroll shop in Río Blanco.

In the first decade from 1900 to 1910, foreign investment had increased to 1,700 million dollars (38% American, 29% English and 27% French). In spite of the fact that, as we have seen, an important labor force already existed, the country was agrarian par excellence: 70% of the populace subsisted from the land. Since the lack of equilibrium continued to increase to the detriment of the poorer classes, imperceptibly all of the above led toward a crisis.

In summary, one may state that there were 11 million peasants, 195,000 laborers and 500,000 artisans. The laborers, which constituted an incipient working class, were concentrated in the large cities such as Mexico City, Monterrey, Puebla, Guadalajara and Veracruz.

Another very important element in the Porfirian society of the time was represented by the army which had undergone great changes due to the fact that the old guard made up of old generals who had fought during the French Intervention (1861-1867) and the so-called Second Empire of Maximilian (1863-1867) were giving way to the formation of a modern one in which the Chapultepec Military School had a determining influence. Outstanding military men were sent to Europe, principally to France, to study the latest innovations. Among them it is sufficient to mention artillery men such as Manuel Mondragón and Felipe Angeles.

Armaments were modernized by acquiring artillery, guns and warships from the principal European powers. Troops continued to be a problem; the recruitment system was that known as "leva", in other words enforced recruitment; the political heads of the towns had a quota to fulfill so they sent to the army units peasants recruited by force or common criminals. At the beginning of the revolution, the Military School turned out trained technical officers, but as yet they were insufficient in number, and the Army High Command was still in the hands of old generals who were friends of the President. There existed also the much feared Rural Brigade which was a police force in charge of maintaining peace and order in rural communities and on many occasions did so by means of brutal methods.

The political situation in Mexico came to a head with the sixth reelection of General Porfirio Díaz. Two years previously Díaz had granted James Greelman, an American journalist from *Pearson Magazine,* an interview which at that time was considered sensational. In this interview the old statesman had given his views on democracy, on his reelection, on the political maturity of the Mexican people, on foreign investments and on many other important subjects.

The interview took place on February 18, 1908, at Chapultepec Castle, the official residence of Mexico's presidents in those years. In said interview he made declarations such as:

"I have awaited patiently the day when the Mexican people would be prepared to select and change their government in each election without the danger of armed revolutions and the obstruction of the progress of the country. I believe that day has come."

Further on he stated with reference to the opposition:

"I would happily welcome an opposition party in the Mexican Republic, if such were to be formed, as a blessing not an evil. And if it were to develop power, not to exploit, but to govern, I would sustain it, advise it and forget about myself, to inaugurate a totally successful democratic government in the Republic."

"It would be enough for me to see Mexico emerge among the useful and peaceful nations. I have no desire to continue in the Presidency. This nation is ready to assume its freedom. At the age of 77 I take satisfaction in enjoying good health."

"As for me I can say in all sincerity, this now long

*President Francisco I. Madero. Apostle of Democracy. Assassinated during the "Decena Trágica" (Tragic Ten Days).*

*José María Pino Suárez, Lawyer. Vice-President of the Republic. Assassinated during the Tragic Ten Days.*

tenure in the Presidency has not corrupted my political ideals. To the contrary, it has helped to convince me more and more that democracy is the only just and true form of government, although in practice it is only feasible for already developed nations."

The above declarations caused a sensation in Mexico and gave a new impetus to the political enemies of the government. Anti-reelection clubs were formed all over the Republic, and leaders and intellectuals began to appear giving their opinions on Mexico's future.

At the end of that year, a book appeared in San Pedro de las Colonias, Coahuila which would be a powerful influence on the events herein chronicled. The book was entitled *The Presidential Succession in 1910* bearing the subtitle "The National Democratic Party". Its author was a wealthy landowner in Coahuila, Don Francisco I. Madero. The book analyzed the political situation of the nation and in it Madero revealed his passionate belief that democracy was the system of government necessary for Mexico. The book of course was critical of Díaz's government, although its tone is moderate. This book greatly influenced the thinking population because this was the first time the necessity of creating a Democratic party had been put into words.

As a result of the statements made to Creelman and the publication of Madero's book, various political parties began to emerge, some supporting the old dictator, others backing the new electoral formula: Díaz for President; Ramón Corral for Vice-President; others in open opposition of everything that reeked of the present regime.

To prepare for the political strife anticipated in 1910, active propaganda was initiated by the Democratic party which included people such as Attorney Benito Juárez Maza, son of the meritorius President Benito Juárez, Manuel Calero, José Peón del Valle, outstanding orators such as Jesús Urueta, Rafael Zubarán Campmany, Diodoro Batalla, and other distinguished professional men and intellectuals. In April 1909, this new party published a Manifesto, in which were concretely expressed aspirations its, some of the principal points of which were:

1. Preservation of peace.
2. Slow evolution, without sudden changes or violence.
3. Respect of life and liberty.
4. The Constitution of 1857 and the Reform Laws to remain in force and effect.
5. Liberty for the Municipal Governments and suppression of political leaders.
6. Autonomy and inmutability of the Judicial Power.
7. Development of education, basis of political progress.
8. Investigation of a new electoral law for the purpose of establishing the direct vote.
9. Organization of a Ministry of Agriculture in order to inaugurate internal credit and agrarian policies.
10. Preparation of a work accident law as a first step toward complete labor legislation.

Another important political group were the royalists who founded the Popular Sovereignty Club; this group supported General Bernardo Reyes, Governor of the State of Morelos, ex-Secretary of War and of the Navy and a military man who enjoyed great prestige in the country. General Bernardo Reyes, who shortly was to play an important role in the events which were to determine the downfall of the Madero government, was a native of Jalisco and Governor of the northern state of Nuevo León, where he installed a progressive government for which he was commended by General Díaz, who during a visit to Monterrey and on the occasion of a toast, made the following remarks in honor of Reyes: "This is the way to govern". As Secretary of War and of the Navy he had performed a commendable job, creating a Second Military Reserve, the Candidates Military School, which had given him fame as an organizer in the army. All of this had made him one of the most popular figures of the moment, and therefore a group of intellectuals, among them personalities such as Dr. Francisco Vázquez Gómez and Attorney José López Portillo y Rojas, had organized the above-mentioned Club, placing on their political ticket the names of Díaz as President and Reyes as Vice-President.

Nevertheless, a short time later, General Reyes was eliminated. General Díaz decided to run again for the period 1910-1914 and also decided that his running mate would be Ramón Corral and not General Reyes, who accepted a post in Europe to which he soon departed.

In 1909 the Reelection Club was reorganized in order to work for the Sixth Reelection of General Díaz. On February 9, 1909, a large number of politicians from the financial world and from the so-called Mexican aristocracy gathered together at the home of General Pedro Rincón Gallardo; among those present were Ignacio Alvarez Icaza, Manuel Iturbide, José Castellot, Joaquín D. Casasús, Manuel Buch, Rafael Dondé, Pedro Gorozpe and many others. Don Jesús Silva Herzog, in his *Brief History of the Mexican Revolution* recounts the following on the Reelection Club. "Mr. López Portillo y Rojas entitled *The Rise and Fall of Porfirio Díaz* upon referring to Mexico City as regards the subject matter states as follows: 'Prominent in the Reelection Club were the better known Scientists (Científicos ... a group of party members very important to President Díaz), the most fervent catholics, men of wealth of sundry views, and even close relatives of the anti-reelection candidate'. And the fact is that the close relatives of Mr. Madero —we should mention— belonged to the moneyed class of the country." In effect such was the case and logically these people could make use of complete official support for their political activities.

On the other hand, in opposition to the reelectionists, there appeared the Anti-Reelection Center in which Mr. Francisco I. Madero, who for some time had worked for the democratic party, figured prominently.

His followers were composed of a very distinguised group of career men and intellectuals such as Messrs. Juan Sánchez Azcona, Emilio Vázquez Gómez, and Toribio Esquivel Obregón, a prominent lawyer. After overcoming many problems, on May 22, 1909, the Center was established in the home of Alfredo Robles Domínguez, an engineer. On that day, in addition to the above-named, present were José Vasconcelos, one of the most distinguished men in Mexico, Félix Palavicini, Filomeno Mata, an intrepid and aggressive journalist, Don Luis Cabrera —one of the most brilliant Revolutionary ideologists— and many more.

The Anti-Reelection Center published the reasons for its formation; among other things mentioned in said treatise are the following:

"The consolidation of Mexican nationality can only be attained through the participation of the people in the Government. For a long time now we have been unable to achieve this participation by the people due to official pressures and the apathy of its citizens, which has permitted public officials to remain indefinitely in power."

"The undefined reelection of the governing officials has as a result the concentration of such an amount of power that it constitutes a menace to the liberties of the people."

"The most efficient means of avoiding the loss of political rights is to make use of them."

Next came the political program which established:

"1. To undertake a broad propaganda program in order to make the people exercise their rights and comply with their duties as citizens.

"2. To promote political conventions to designate candidates and to discuss general principles of government which the latter should uphold.

"3. To organize the Anti-Reelection Party throughout the Republic and establish local centers which support our objectives.

"4. To instigate citizens to take part in the electoral campaigns and especially in the future elections for President and Vice-President, Deputies and municipal authorities, in order to obtain a wider choice of public officials.

"5. In the execution of its program, this Party has no other purpose but that of serving the great interests of the Nation and to accomplish this it will avail itself of the majority of all good Mexicans. It shall not hesitate to enter into agreements or make alliances with all other National Political parties."

The signers among others were Emilio Vázquez Gómez and Don Francisco I. Madero. But who was Mr. Madero? This singular man was born on October 30, 1873, in Hacienda "El Rosario", Coahuila, the son and grandson of landowners. Mr. Madero was brought up in wealthy surroundings. He studied in France where he remained for five years. After returning to Mexico, he became interested in the political problems of the country. He wrote a book entitled *The Presidential Succession,* which had a great deal of influence at that time in Mexico. He then decided to join the struggle against the reelection of General Díaz. A short time later, he was to become the principal figure in the cause which brought him to the Presidency of the Republic in the midst of the authentic civic enthusiasm of the Mexican people, which seldom had been seen. Victim of a coup d'état, he was assassinated on February 22, 1913.

In his book *Madero and Pino Suárez,* Andrés Iduarte describes him in the following manner: "Of light complexion, bearded, small in stature, inspired by faith, as good as gold, humble as St. Francis, he has always reminded me of David: his deep faith overcame Goliath, giant of the dictatorship. At the service of the people's cause, he placed his fortunes and his very life and that of those close to him. What I most remember of him is his smile and the sweetness of his voice even for his friends. The rays of sunshine were never lacking in his struggle, but even in his ardor there existed the tenderness of creation, the warmth of the hearth. No one ever made more dispassionate or just comments to the Dictator, and even up to the last moment without limitation called his attention to the truth with the most serene, lucid and cordial reasoning, in defiance of those men of violence who were unable to achieve the highest strength in man. No one has yet determined how much bloodshed he avoided, although there was much shed; the miraculous game between admonition and combat, the kind of admonition which did not refrain but strengthened the battle. In this he never made use of hate, because he did not feel hate, because it was unknown to him, for he had left it behind in the remote beginnings of the common man. Nor did he believe in the power of revenge for he had come precisely to banish it. Enveloped in the light of the benefactor, under its guidance he galloped unflinchingly, fearlessly, and in this same light he died without weakness.

Finally, there remained only two parties, face to face: the powerful Reelectionist party and the young and idealistic Anti-Reelectionist party, and both prepared for the electoral campaign.

Mr. Madero initiated a campaign throughout the country trying to inject new spirit and to make the people see the need of overcoming their disinterest and their political apathy, to fight against the oppressive measures of the Government which presented many difficulties in the cities which he visited. As an example, let us mention what occurred in Colima. Professor Jesús Romero Flores, a distinguished constituent in 1917, historian and politician, in his treatise "Annals of the Mexican Revolution", writes: "He first encountered open hostility in Colima. He was forbidden to print circulars announcing his meetings to the people; he was also denied locations to hold these meetings, and finally, with the intervention of the police, he was not permitted to be heard by his sympathizers."

The political struggle continued to the great disadvantage of the Apostle of Democracy. Finally, at the petition of a San Luis Potosí District Judge, Mr. Madero and Roque Estrada were arrested in Monterrey, accused of inciting the people to rebellion. Madero was returned to San Luis and imprisoned in the State Penitentiary. After 45 days in jail he was given his freedom under bond but incarcerated within the boundaries of the city of San Luis.

The elections took place on June 26th and, as was to be expected, Messrs. Díaz and Corral were elected for the new term of government (1910-1914).

On October 6 Mr. Madero was able to escape from San Luis Potosí and headed for San Antonio where he was soon joined by his family and a group of his close friends among which were Sánchez Azcona, González Garza, and others.

*A group of pro-Félix rebels firing from the Ciudadela (Citadel) during the Tragic Ten Days. February 1913.*

Madero was able to escape because he was not watched very closely. The distinguished historian Don Jesús Silva Herzog, in his above-mentioned book, confirms this declaring: "The author of this book saw him, on more than one occasion, strolling in the public park which is located in front of the railroad station. I was never aware, nor did I observe, that he was closely watched".

The document known as the Plan of San Luis was published on October 5, 1910, in the City of San Luis Potosí, although actually it was written in San Antonio, Texas. In this document the election of the President and the Vice-President of the Republic as well as the magistrates of the Supreme Court of the Nation and deputies and senators which took place in June, was declared null and void. Article Third, in the opinion of Silva Herzog, is the most important of the Plan due to the significance it had for the rural community of Mexico. This Article states: "By violating the law regarding public lands, numerous small landowners, mainly Indians, have been stripped of their properties by decrees of the Department of Land Development or by judicial decisions of the Courts of the Republic. Since it is only just that the lands of which they were deprived so arbitrarily be restored to their previous owners, such decrees and judicial decisions are declared subject to revision, and those persons who acquired them so immorally, or their heirs, shall be required to restore them to their previous owners, and they shall also be asked to pay an indemnization for the damages caused. Only in cases where these lands have been transferred to third parties before the publication of this Plan, shall the original owners receive indemnization from those parties in whose benefit the eviction was carried out." The historian Silva Herzog correctly judged that this article was a determining factor in motivating Emiliano Zapata and his people to join the struggle in view of the fact that in Morelos there was actual evidence of such evictions.

In the Plan of San Luis, Don Francisco I. Madero was acknowledged as Provisional President and Leader of the Revolution, and vindications of a social nature were insisted upon because it was affirmed that: "All property appropriated in order to give it to the people favored by the present administration shall be returned to the original owners." Also, the injustices suffered by the indigenous population for many centuries were acknowledged, as it was stated that: "The Indian race shall be protected in every way, endeavoring in every way possible to uphold its dignity and promote its prosperity."

Future social benefits for laborers were established, and it was determined that: "The work-day for laborers of both sexes shall be lengthened both in the field and in the city." "Work hours shall be no less than eight, nor more than nine." November 20 was designated as the date on which all citizens of the Republic should take up arms to overthrow the authorities who were actually in power at that time.

Also on that date Madero signed another Manifesto addressed to the Federal Army inviting it to join the revolutionary movement.

The country was ripe for the Revolution; already years before there had been some frustrated attempts at revolt against the Government of General Díaz. The most important occurred on June 24, 1908, in the town of Viesca, Coahuila where Benito Ibarra, accompanied by a few faithful men, took up arms against General Díaz; on June 26 another uprising took place in Palomas, Chihuahua led by Enrique Flores Magón; José Inés Salazar, Práxedis Guerrero and others repudiated the government following the principles of Ricardo Flores Magón who was in St. Louis Missouri, U.S.A. These small uprisings, unconnected and disorganized, were easily suppressed by the Government. More important were the events which took place in the city of Valladolid, Yucatán where a group of people, discontent with the political boss Luis Felipe Regil, assassinated him, provoking a strong repression, as the principal leaders such as Maximilian R. Bonilla, Atilano Albertos and José E. Kantún were sentenced to death and shot on June 25th in the patio of a church. Gabriel Leyva took up arms in Sinaloa, but his attempt failed and he was captured by federal troops and shot.

The most serious of all the uprisings occurred in the city of Puebla where Aquiles Serdán with the help of his family launched an attack from his home on November 18th and was cut down by bullets; hidden in his home, he was discovered and killed on the dawn of November 19th by Lieutenant Porfirio Pérez. In spite of all this, revolts were initiated in some parts of the Republic in accordance with orders given by Madero. These occurred principally in rural areas. Pascual Orozco and Francisco Villa rose in rebellion in Chihuahua, José M. Maytorena, Eulalio Gutiérrez and Luis Gutiérrez in Coahuila, Jesús Agustín Castro in Gómez Palacio, Durango, Cesáreo Castro in Cuatro Ciénegas, Coahuila, in Cuchillo Parado, Chihuahua, José de la Luz Blanco, Luis Moya in Zacatecas, the Figueroa brothers in Guerrero, and in the State of Morelos, Emiliano Zapata, The battle camps were defined: the Mexican nation made ready for a fight to the death against the old dictatorship in order to change an unjust way of life.

In synthesis, we can say that the reasons for the conflict were, according to Attorney Luis Cabrera (Blas Urrea, Complete Works), the following:

CACIQUISM (BOSSISM): Concretely, the despotic oppression practiced by local authorities having direct contact with the proletarian classes; this harassment is made possible because of existing arbitrary procedures, such as the fugitive law (Murder committed by government agents in which it is made to appear that the prisoner has tried to escape for which reason the agents are forced to shoot him) and many other forms of hostility and obstruction of the right to make a living.

LABOR GANGS: The de facto slavery or feudal servitude endured by the day laborer, above all a laborer engaged or deported from the southeastern area of the country, a system which subsists due to economic, political or judicial privileges enjoyed by the landowner.

LABOR CONTROL SYSTEM (FABRIQUISMO): Personal and economic servitude which the factory worker has in fact submitted himself to, due to the privileged position which the landlord enjoys economically and politically as a result of the systematic protection which it is believed necessary to make available to industry.

LAND CONTROL SYSTEM (HACENDISMO): The economic pressure and unfair competition which the large agrarian landholder exerts over the small landholder as a result of disparity in taxation and the many economic and political privileges enjoyed by the former, which have as a consequence the constant absorption of small agrarian properties by big ones.

COMMERCIAL CONTROL SYSTEM (CIENTIFI-CISMO): The commercial and financial monopoly and the unfair competition exerted by big business over small business, as a result of the official protection and political influence which government officials can make available to big business.

FOREIGN CONTROL SYSTEM (EXTRANJERIS-MO): The domination and unfair protection exerted in all types of activities by foreigners over Mexican nationals, as a result of their privileged position due to the excessive protection which they enjoy from the authorities and the support and viligance of their diplomatic representatives.

# 2

The Revolution of 1910-1911. Revolts of the Zapata brothers in Morelos. Principal military operations in Chihuahua. Ciudad Juárez falls into the hands of the revolutionaries. The Ciudad Juárez treaties. Resignations of General Díaz and Corral. Interim government of President Francisco León de la Barra. Triumphant entry of Madero into Mexico City.

It was in the vast northern state of Chihuahua where military operations against the government of General Díaz were initiated. The first encounter between the revolutionaries commanded by Pascual Orozco and the troops of the Third Cavalry Regiment led by Captain Salvador Ormachea took place on November 21st in Ciudad Guerrero, Chihuahua. As a result of this action, the army sent troops against Ciudad Guerrero, 160 men of the Twelfth Batallion arriving to reinforce the garrison. In Chihuahua, the strength of the revolution was Abraham González, who is described by Attorney Isidro Fabela in the following manner: "Don Abraham was a strong man, tall, robust, a bit paunchy, broad-shouldered, his complexion was tawny, but not too dark, he had a thick greying moustache which he never neglected, a broad forehead, a straight nose, a well-defined mouth with thin lips, large, very dark eyes, thick eyebrows and a lively look. Taken as a whole, his face was an interesting one; it revealed at the same time both an energetic character and kindness; and in his glance, which was always alert, glittered a brilliant light: intelligence. His voice was pleasant, soft in tone and clearly modulated. His laughter was frank and sonorous like that of a child. He walked erectly and calmly with the firm and sure gait of a man in command."

The above, in outline, describes the leader of the revolution in Northern Mexico. His principal followers were Pascual Orozco and Francisco (Pancho) Villa.

General Pascual Orozco, formerly a muleteer, was one of the principal revolutionary military figures in Chihuahua. He is described by Rafael F. Muñoz in the following manner: "Pascual Orozco was a skinny man, tall and slim, whose bone structure revealed a vigor created not by athletic games, but by an agile and robust life in the fields, the rustic tasks he undertook, his incessant communion with nature, and the spontaneous vitality given to a man, not unlike a tree, when he develops in the very bosom of nature." Further on Muñoz declares: "He was not one to do much talking, quite to the contrary, he was reticent, timid, and of a sober mien, and never lent a ready ear to confi-

*President Madero arriving at Constitution Plaza, accompanied by cadets from the Military College, upon initiating the uprising in February 1913.*

dences, but those who have seen him fight, who were his companions during the Revolution, affirm that he was rapid and sure in action, vigorous and constant, and that his bravery was inexhaustible and prudent."

Many books have been written about Pancho Villa. He was a man who will always be discussed; admired up to the point of exaggeration, execrated by others to the point of infamy. His real name was Doroteo Arango, and he was born June 5, 1878, in a rural community known as La Coyotada, in the municipality of San Juan del Río, Durango. A passionate man, he has become a legend, and without a doubt, he was one of the great leaders of the Revolution. As a military man, he is described as follows by General Miguel A. Sánchez Lamego: "General Villa, who possessed little or no education, was impulsive, haughty, tenacious and cruel. He exercised his command by means of violence and fear: thus, for example, to induce his subordinates to comply with the missions he entrusted to them, he threatened them with death if they were unable to complete them". Marte R. Gómez, an engineer, in his *Villa, An Attempt at a Biographical Sketch,* among other things, describes him thus as a guerrilla: "In addition, he was clever, gifted with enormous resources to handle small contingents of men inured to war and capable of travelling great distances at full gallop, appearing and disappearing in an unreasonable manner in the most unlikely places, characteristics so peculiar that they garnered him resplendent victories and gave birth to the aureola which consecrated him as a guerrilla without equal." Further on Gómez states (page 67): "Villa possessed a personal magnetism which permitted him to attract thousands of men to follow him and join the ranks of his famous and experienced División del Norte (Northern Division). There is no doubt that he had authority to command, and no one argues the point. Unfortunately his pride, completely out of bounds, impelled him to try to take command of everything and everyone. That is why he never, nor before anyone, agreed to recognize any other authority but his own. On many occasions he lost himself in the mires of violence, acting solely on impulse."

These men were in synthesis the principal leaders of the Madero movement in Chihuahua at the end of 1910 and the beginning of 1911. Orozco, after the battle in Ciudad Guerrero, went to Pedernales, Chihuahua, where he entered into battle with federal troops in which he was victorious. On November 30th he returned to Ciudad Guerrero and captured the city.

On December 15, 1910, Villa was ousted from the town of San Andrés by federal troops under the command of Lieutenant Colonel Agustín Martínez. Subsequently, he had an encounter with the troops of General Navarro, retreating toward Parral. General Díaz, from Mexico, took over the command of operations, aided by his son Porfirio and Colonel Samuel García Cuéllar. They ordered General Juan Navarro to recapture Ciudad Guerrero. The latter obeyed marching with the 20th Infantry Batallion. The attack was undertaken with extreme precaution, sustaining skirmishes with the forces of Orozco in Cerro Prieto and finally establishing headquarters in Pedernales. There he awaited the reinforcement led by Colonel Martín Luis Guzmán (father of the famous writer who bore the same name). Since the troops had to cross the Mal Paso Canyon, General Navarro sent a column of 475 men commanded by Colonel Fernando Trucy Aubert to rid the canyon of possible enemies, an event which in effect took place. The battle which ensued lasted six hours, at the end of which the Madero forces commanded by Pascual Orozco and J. de la Luz Blanco retreated. Two days later, on December 18th, a second encounter took place in Mal Paso. On this occasion the revolutionaries took the federal forces by surprise and sustained a battle which lasted four-and-a-half hours. Colonel Guzmán ordered the retreat upon perceiving the superiority in number of the revolutionary forces. There were three injured leaders in the federal troops: Colonel Guzmán himself, who died December 29th in the City of Chihuahua, the then Major Vito Alessio Robles (future politician and distinguished historian) and Lieutenant Colonel Vallejo.

The Government, after this failure, ordered reinforcements for Navarro's troops, which was done, and in this manner the General was able to renew his attack, occupying Ciudad Guerrero on January 6th without combat, as it had been evacuated by Orozco and his men.

In other parts of the Republic the growing revolution was spreading. In Zacatecas Luis Moya rose in rebellion in the town of Nieves and defeated Major Ismael Ramos in Aguaje, Durango and a short time later he took the town of San Juan de Guadalupe. A bold man, he took part in a brief campaign in Zacatecas, but was killed in battle on May 11th of that year in the town of Sombrerete.

In Sonora, Salvador Alvarado and Juan G. Cabral, with their followers, occupied Cuquiarachi, and continued their march to Frontera and Bacoachi. In Sahuaripa, Severiano Talamantes rose in rebellion; in Chihuahua, an old follower of the socialist leader Ricardo Flores Magón, Práxedis Guerrero, rose in rebellion in Janos, Chihuahua, but he did not have much luck as he was killed by federal troops. In Baja California another follower of Flores Magón, José M. Leyva, commanding a small group of rebels captured Mexicali, although it was of short duration because a group of American adventurers joined the movement, an event which lessened the merit of the revolution.

In view of the above situation, Mr. Francisco Madero who, as we may recall, was in San Antonio, Texas, decided to return to Mexican territory, again settling in the outskirts of Zaragoza (15 kilometers southeast of Ciudad Juárez). On February 14, 1911, he was joined by Abraham González, who had been designated Provisional Governor of Chihuahua, Engineer Eduardo Hay, who functioned as the Head of the General Staff, José de la Luz Soto, designated Colonel of the Liberating Army, his brother Raúl Madero, the Boer General Benjamín Viljoen, José Garibaldi, grandson of the Italian hero and a numerous group of followers, both Mexican as well as American. With these men he went to the town of Guadalupe. The news of his arrival spread rapidly, both among his followers as well as among as also among the supporters of the government. Madero decided to attack the town of Casas Grandes, Chihuahua, defended by Colonel Agustín Valdez (Commander of the 18th Infantry Batalion), the garrison consisting of some 500 men. On March 6th, leading 800 men, all of them irregulars, he ordered the attack, which failed, thanks to the opportune arrival of federal reinforcements commanded by Colonel Samuel García Cuéllar (Head of the President's General Staff). The revolutionaries retreated in defeat. Mr. Madero himself, leader of the Revolution, had received a wound in the arm. Also wounded was Colonel García Cuéllar, a leader of the federal troops.

Mr. Madero, after this defeat, withdrew in order to reorganize his forces, and little by little received the reinforcements from different parties operating in the States, among them those of Pascual Orozco and Pancho Villa, the number of new allies growing to more than 1,500 men.

With these men he planned to attack the capital of the State, but later he changed his mind and decided to attack Ciudad Juárez, an important frontier town where the most important Customs House was located and situated near El Paso, an American city in the State of Texas. The garrison at Ciudad Juárez was under the command of Infantry Colonel Manuel Tamborrell, who had organized some defensive maneuvers with the aid of Fortino Dávila, Lieutenant Colonel in the General Staff's Special Corps. The command of all the troops was assigned to General Juan C. Navarro who arrived from Ciudad Guerrero to take charge of the city's defense. The revolutionaries, commanded by Orozco and Villa, attacked the city on May 8th and 9th, and after a furious battle, they defeated the federal troops. General Navarro decided to surrender with the forces at his command. Among the dead were Colonel Tamborrell, who had been a distinguished student of the Chapultepec Military School. On May 17th an armistice was signed for a period of five days, which included all Mexican territory. Finally on May 21st a new Peace Treaty was concluded and signed in that city.

Meanwhile, let us regress a bit, to follow important events in Mexico City. Here, General Díaz, disillusioned and sickly, burdened by the onslaughts of old age, as he was 80 years old, decided to make important changes in his cabinet with the hope of detaining the Revolutión. Nevertheless, in one of the most important posts which was the War Office, he permitted the same old General González Cosío to remain, and refused to accept the recommendation of naming his old protégé, General Bernardo Reyes, who could have injected new life into the federal troops. With his new cabinet, on April 1st he appeared before the National Congress where he read his report in which he manifested his desire to respect suffrage and establish the principle of no reelection. It was too late because the Revolution was already putting him out of office. The government named Attorney Francisco Carbajal as its representative to deal with the revolutionaries; on behalf of the latter, Doctor Vázquez Gómez, Attorney José M. Pino Suárez and Francisco Madero, Sr. were named. The initial negotiations failed. On May 7th, shortly before the fall of Ciudad Juárez, General Porfirio Díaz issued a Manifesto addressed to the people of Mexico, which read:

"The rebellion initiated in Chihuahua, in November of last year which because of the cragginess of the land we were unable to suppress in time, has stirred up the anarchist tendencies and the spirit of adventure in other regions of the Republic, always latent in some social spheres of our country. The Government I preside, responded, as was its strict duty, by combating the armed movement in military and political order. The President of the Republic, in his report rendered before the Congress of the Union, on April 1st last, declared before the entire nation, and above all, before the civilized world, that it was his purpose to enter a path of political and administrative reforms, in obeisance to the just and opportune demands of public opinion. It is well known that the Government, ignoring the charge against it of not acting spontaneously, but due to the pressure of the rebellion, has put all its efforts into bringing about the reforms which have been promised."

The closing paragraphs were more dramatic and demonstrated the desire of General Díaz to avoid more bloodshed and his decision to resign if necessary, but with the necessary dignity and decorum. These paragraphs declared:

"The President of the Republic, whose painful duty it is to address himself to the people in these solemn moments, will resign, yes, from power, but in a manner convenient to a nation which is respected, as is the prerogative of a leader who may have undoubtedly committed errors, but who on the other hand has known how to defend his country and serve it with loyalty."

After the fall of the city, as we have indicated, on May 8th and 9th, Madero, in his position as Provisional President, decided to name his cabinet, with the following persons: Secretary of the Interior, Federico González Garza; Secretary of State, Doctor Francisco Vázquez Gómez; Justice Department, Attorney José M. Pino Suárez; Engineer Manuel Bonilla in Communications and Mr. Venustiano Carranza in War and Navy. As a result of the fall of Ciudad Juárez, Mr. Madero gave a firm example of his kindness, of the many he would give later, by defending the defeated General Navarro from the anger of Orozco and Villa who wanted to have him shot. In spite of the insistence of these revolutionary leaders, Madero took General Navarro to the neighboring city of El Paso. This had as a result that the two above-mentioned generals rebelled and wanted to kill Madero. The latter, when he discovered what they were planning, delivered a speech to his troops warning them of the danger. Obviously the above events enormously increased Mr. Madero's popularity.

The downfall of this important city, constituted a moral victory rather than a military triumph, because it must be considered that the federal army was practically intact; but the capture of Ciudad Juárez shattered the Mexican people, who realized that it was possible to defeat General Díaz. Doctor Francisco Vázquez Gómez so states in his Political Memoirs: "Evidently I agree that the seizure of Ciudad Juárez, without causing an international incident, contrib-

*General Victoriano Huerta together with*
*General Téllez, at the Bachimba*
*battles, during the rebellion*
*of Pascual Orozco. 1912.*

uted greatly to the triumph of the Revolution; more so, due to its moral influence than to its military importance. Don Ramón Prida in his book *From Dictatorship to Anarchy* gives the following opinion:

"The defeat of Ciudad Juárez was a coup de grace to the Government of General Díaz. With one lone battle won, with the capture of a city of such small importance such as Ciudad Juárez, the revolution initiated in November 1910 had triumphed". It was not force but public opinion which triumphed. Even though this was true, it should also be taken into account that General Díaz, in a show of patriotism, did not wish to provoke or prolong a bloody civil war, or possible foreign intervention, for we must not forget a most important point, and this is that the Porfirian Government did not have the blessing of the United States. Díaz's Government had given many signs of political independence: it had been opposed to the lease of Magdalena Bay in Baja California; it had provoked the ire of the United States when it sent a Mexican gunboat to the port of Corinto, Nicaragua to pick up General Santos Celaya, the President deposed by the Americans in that Central American Republic. Due to all of the above, we should not discard a possible intervention which would have provoked a new international war. Due to the above-described circumstances, the President decided to present his irrevocable resignation. Finally, on May 21, 1911, an important Peace Treaty was signed which stated:

"In Ciudad Juárez on the 21st of May nineteen hundred eleven, in the building of the Border Customs Office, Attorney Francisco S. Carbajal, representative of the Government, General Porfirio Díaz, Don Francisco Vázquez Gómez, Don Francisco Madero and Attorney José María Pino Suárez, the three latter representing the revolution, met to deal with the manner of ceasing hostilities in all parts of Mexican territory, considering:

"First. That General Porfirio Díaz has declared his resolution to resign the Presidency of the Republic, before the end of this month;

"Second. That there is bonafide evidence that Mr. Ramón Corral will also resign the Vice Presidency of the Republic within the same period of time;

"Third. That by means of the powers granted by law, Attorney Don Francisco León de la Barra, actual Secretary of Foreign Affairs in the Government of General Díaz, shall take charge provisionally of the Executive Power of the Nation, and shall convoke general elections in accordance with the terms of the Constitution;

"Fourth. That the new Government will study the consensus of public opinion as of the present time to satisfy it in each State within the constitutional order and shall make the corresponding resolutions to pay the indemnizations for the damages caused directly by the Revolution.

"The two parties represented in this conference, due to the above considerations, have agreed to formalize this agreement.

"SOLE AGREEMENT. From this day forward all hostilities which have existed between the forces of General Díaz's Government and those of the Revolution, shall cease in the entire territory of the Mexican Republic; the militia should be discharged in accordance with the manner in which each State takes the necessary steps to reestablish and guarantee peace and public order.

"TRANSITORY CLAUSE. Immediate action shall be taken of course to proceed with the reconstruction and repair of the telegraph lines and railroads which are presently interrupted.

"This agreement is signed in duplicate.

*Francisco S. Carbajal*

*Francisco Madero, Sr.*

*Francisco Vázquez Gómez*

*José M. Pino Suárez*

(Signatures)"

Events now took place at great speed, and there occurred what we have seen take place many times before in many countries. The masses, previously respectful of the Government, in those moments of uncontrolled anarchy attacked the business shops and government offices of the city violently, demonstrating in this way their desires repressed for so many years. In diverse parts of the Republic, similar manifestations took place. In Mexico City, thanks to the good offices of Engineer Alfredo Robles Domínguez, representative of the Revolution in Mexico City, the excesses were able to be controlled.

On May 25th, the long-awaited resignation of the Chamber of Deputies finally arrived along with that of Ramón Corral, up to that time the Vice-President. Due to the transcendental importance of this document in the history of modern Mexico, we reproduce it below:

"TO THE SECRETARIES OF THE HONORABLE CHAMBER OF DEPUTIES.

"To be personally delivered.

"The Mexican nation, that nation which has so generously bestowed me with honors, which proclaimed me its leader during the War of Intervention, which patriotically supported me in all the projects undertaken to foment industry and commerce in the Republic, that nation, honorable deputies, has rebelled in armed militant bands, manifesting that my presence in the office of Supreme Executive of the Nation is the reason for the rebellion.

"I am unaware of any act imputable to me which could have motivated this social phenomenon, but allowing, without conceding, that I may be unconsciously guilty, such possibility makes my person the least qualified to argue and express an opinion as to my own culpability.

"For this reason, respecting, as I have always respected the will of the people, and in accordance with Article 82 of the Federal Constitution, I come before the Supreme Body of this Nation, to resign the office I hold as Constitutional President of the Republic with which this nation has honored me. I do so for the potent reason that if I were to try to retain it, it would be necessary to shed more Mexican blood, debasing the good name of the nation, squandering its riches, stopping up its resources and exposing its political future to international conflicts.

"It is my expectation, honorable deputies, that once the passions accompanying all revolutions are assuaged, a more conscientious and verified investigation will bring forth in the national conscience, a correct judgment which will permit me to die, carrying with me in the depths of my soul, a just compensation for the esteem which all my life I have dedicated and will continue to dedicate to my compatriots."

"With all respect.

"Mexico, May 25, 1911.

*"Porfirio Díaz (Signature)"*

The following day, Madero published a Manifesto to the Nation. We have selected some of the more interesting paragraphs, in which he stated:

"FELLOW MEXICANS:

"When I invited you to take up arms, I told you to be invincible in war and magnanimous in victory. You have faithfully complied with my recommendations, winning the world's admiration. Well now I recommend that just as you knew how to clutch your weapons to defend your rights, that you continue to clutch them in the role of national sentinels. You must place yourselves on the level of your new duties which consist of keeping order and representing a guarantee to the new society and the new order of things; that you retire to private life, and wield the new weapon that you have acquired: the vote. Use this most powerful weapon freely and very soon you will see that it will offer you more important and durable victories than those with which your rifles provided you. . ."

The solution given after the victory of the Revolution, was not satisfactory to some of Madero's followers; they wanted to break away completely from the old order. They did not desire a transition such as the one which in effect had taken place, and one reason for this was that Provisional President, Francisco León de la Barra, was a well-known supporter of the Porfirian Regime. Logically, he would more or less follow the same order of things. Attorney Luis Cabrera, one of the most notable ideologists of the Revolution, sent him a letter which among other things stated: "Revolutions are always exceedingly painful operations to the social body. However, a surgeon is not required to heal the wound before removing the gangrene.

The operation, necessary or not, has commenced. You opened the wound and you are obliged to heal it. May God forgive you if you are daunted by the sight of blood or disturbed by the painful lamentations of our country. If the wound were to be healed hastily without disinfecting it, or rooting out the evil which it was your purpose to eradicate, the sacrifice will have been in vain, and history will curse your name, not only for opening the wound, but because the nation would continue to suffer the same evils which it had believed already cured, and, in addition, would be exposed to relapses even more dangerous and threatened with new operations more trying and ever more painful.

"In other words, and to avoid metaphors, you who provoked the Revolution are obliged to squelch it. But God have pity on you, if frightened by bloodshed and softened by the pleas of relatives or threatened by the Yankees, you permit the sacrifices made to bear no fruit. The country will continue to suffer the same evils. It would be exposed to ever more critical crises, and once on the path to the revolution, of which you have been the teacher, it would want to rise up in arms to conquer each of the liberties which would remain unreachable". Attorney Cabrera unfortunately foresaw with keen exactness what would happen in Mexico. At the death of Mr. Madero, there occurred an exceedingly prolonged period of political upheavals which caused many deaths, suffering, misery and frustration to the Mexican people.

The activities of the Zapata brothers in the State of Morelos merit a separate commentary as, even though their rebellion, from the military point of view, did not have a similar importance to that of the revolutionaries in northern Mexico, it did have enormous impact from the social point of view because Zapata represented the ardent desire for social justice of the men who tilled the soil all over the Republic.

Zapata's rebellion took place in the small State of Morelos, very near the capital of the Republic and, precisely because of its small size, the rural problems were considerable. There were enormous sugar plantations in the hands of rich landowners who usually resided in Mexico City, as well as tiny agrarian properties, reduced to the essentials, with land of poor quality wherein the peons could barely eke out a living, in spite of their already frugal requirements. These lands, before the Spanish conquest, had belonged to the people and for centuries had been handed over traditionally to their owners. However, on many occasions the government, or rich landowners, with political influence in government circles, forced or obligated the peons to turn them over to them. Of semi-tropical climate, the region soon converted itself into one of the principal places for the production of sugar. The sugar plantations were scattered due to the limited geography of the State. Morelos in 1910 produced one-third of Mexico's sugar output. Seventeen families were the owners of the principal estates in Morelos. Among them there abounded aristocratic and historical surnames such as Ignacio de la Torre y Mier, García Pimentel, Delfín Sánchez (a descendent of Juárez), Emanuel Amor, Vélez Goríbar, Escandón, Pasquel and many others. These seventeen families possessed a total of 189,070 hectares which produced 52,266,135 kilograms of sugar. The above circumstances and the limited workdays, created discontent, both in Morelos and in the neighboring State of Guerrero where the Figueroa brothers had shown signs of inconformity and had disowned the Government of General Díaz. To the above should be added the political situation. Morelos was ruled by favorites of General

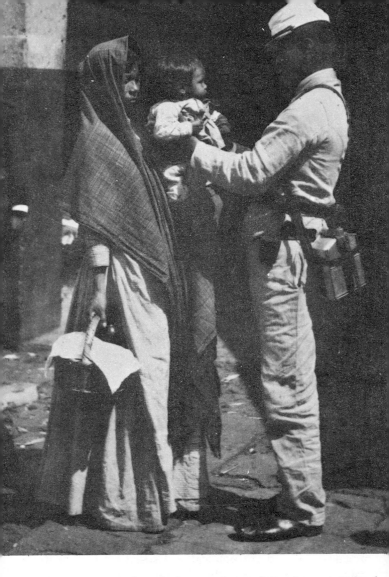

*A typical scene from those days. A federal soldier bids farewell to his small child, who is in the arms of a "soldadera" (woman camp-follower/soldier).*

Díaz, such as Lieutenant Colonel Pablo Escandón. All this created a fertile atmosphere for the Revolution in Morelos. The hungry people, victims of secular injustices, impatiently awaited the moment when someone would rise up in rebellion, and that someone was Emiliano Zapata, who was born in 1877 in the small town of Anenecuilco. (Since the archives of the Public Registry Office in Anenecuilco and Villa de Ayala were destroyed, it is impossible to determine the exact date of his birth). While still a young child, he began to work in the fields, and from that tender age, he became aware of the manner in which the rich landowners, in close combination with the judges, deprived the people of their best public lands. Finally, Villa de Ayala and Anenecuilco, the town of his birth, became the targets of this unlawful practice. Zapata, now a full-grown man, went to Mexico to avoid the loss of the lands of his birthplace. Convinced of the futility of his efforts, he called on his companions to defend with force what could not be defended by legal means. The reaction of the government was the one it utilized at that time for all rural rebellions. They were recruited for the army by means of the disgraceful system of "levying" (forced recruitment) and, therefore, Zapata was taken to the barracks of the Ninth Cavalry Regiment. Thanks to the influence of some aristocrats, he only remained in the army for six months. But already branded a rebel, he had to leave his birthplace and go to work in the State of Puebla. He returned to Morelos in 1909 to be present at the elections for governor. Logically, Escandón, the official candidate, was elected and this only brought to a head the political and social tensions of the State. At the beginning of the Madero Revolution, Morelos became aware of the Plan of San Luis, and especially of Article Third which revealed the injustices against the peons;

this caused a great impact among the dissenters who immediately decided to rebel. On February 7, 1911, Gabriel Tepepa rose up in arms in Tlalquitenango, a town near Jojutla, a very important commercial city. Days later, he was followed by Pablo Torres Burgos and Emiliano Zapata, among others who immediately began to organize the motley mobs, which lacked any type of organization, weapons (except for clumsily-made rifles) or adequate ammunition. All of the above they made up for with their enthusiasm and firm decision to fight, even if they lost their lives, in order to find a solution to their terrible problems. The fighting began, sporadic, unconnected, lacking any type of military tactics, but they began to cause problems to the federal troops stationed there. In Jolalpan, on April 22nd, a meeting was held of all the revolutionary heads, in which they agreed to name Emiliano Zapata as the revolutionary leader in Morelos. At that time the 29th Infantry Division was commanded by Aureliano Blanquet operating in Morelos. This battalion and its commander would have much to do with this story some years later upon the death of Mr. Madero. During the Madero revolution, Zapata fought with varied fortunes against the federal troops, taking part in actions against the towns of Jonacatepec, Cuautla, and others. The resignation of General Díaz had as a consequence the end of hostilities in the State of Morelos and the designation of a provisional Governor, Juan H. Carreón, who had been the General Manager of the Bank of Morelos and who took office on June 2, 1911. Days before, on May 28th, Emiliano Zapata had occupied the city of Cuernavaca.

On June 6th, Zapata travelled to the capital of the Republic for an interview with the leader of the Revolution, Madero. There, at the private home of the Head of the

Revolution, they had a discussion and Madero insisted on the necessity of dismissing the southern troops, taking into account that the Revolution was over. Zapata did not take kindly to this suggestion and made a few objections, which resulted in Madero promising to go to Morelos to study the situation at the actual site of events. This was done, and on June 12th Madero arrived in Cuernavaca, but they were unable to reach an agreement. Zapata never trusted Madero and did not accept his proposal. Nevertheless, they had not as yet come to a breach in their relations and Zapata's troops were disbanded in the presence of the government's representative, Alfredo Robles Domínguez. The rich landowners were not in agreement with the situation in Morelos and began intrigues in high government circles which finally resulted in the decision of Provisional President De la Barra, to again send troops to Morelos. On August 9th Brigadier General Victoriano Huerta was ordered to march to Morelos, taking with him infantry, cavalry and artillery troops or battalions in order to finish the disbanding of the Zapata followers in other parts of Morelos. Madero intervened, trying to solve the differences, with the aid of his brother Gustavo. Everyone wished that when Madero assumed the Presidency, the Republic would be at peace. Again Engineer Robles Domínguez tried to mediate, but was unable to arrive at a solution and Zapata rebelled against the government. It should be noted that he was constantly provoked, and that he finally took up arms in response to these provocations. Zapata, followed by his faithful supporters, arrived at the outskirts of Puebla to join other southern leaders such as Jesús Morales, Francisco Mendoza, and others. There in Ayoxustla, a lonely village in the mountain range bearing the same name, on November 28, 1911, the Plan of Ayala was issued, the author of which was an obscure country teacher, Otilio E. Montaño. This plan was the bible of the Zapatist movement, because it condensed in two words the centuries-old aspiration of the peons all over Mexico: LAND and LIBERTY. In those two words were synthesized the aspiration of millions of destitute people, oppressed by social injustice and at that moment anxious to put an end to the situation.

The Plan disavowed Mr. Madero as the Head of the Revolution and as President of the Republic. The acknowledged head of the Revolution, according to the Plan, was General Pascual Orozco.

Some of the important articles which give an idea of the essence of the Plan are the following:

"Article Sixth. As an additional part of the plan which we invoke, we wish to make clear that property real estate, such as lands, mountains and waters, confiscated by landowners, "científico" or "caciques" in the shadow of tyranny and mercenary justice, will of course revert back to the towns or citizens who have the corresponding deeds of property and were evicted from them as a consequence of the bad faith of our oppressors, who at all cost and bearing arms have kept them; the evictors who believe they have a right to the properties shall plead for them before special courts which will be established when the Revolution triumphs."

"Article Seventh. In view of the fact that the overwhelming majority of Mexican people and citizens are owners merely of the soil upon which they tread, suffering abject poverty without being able to improve their social condition in any way or without being able to dedicate themselves to industry or to agriculture as the land, mountanis and waters are all monopolized by a few persons, these monopolies shall be expropriated from their powerful owners after indemnization is paid in the amount of one-third of their value, so that Mexican people and citizens can acquire legal communal lands, colonies and rural properties for use as towns or as farmland for sowing and working, in order that the prosperity and well-being of Mexicans might improve in every sense." Here we leave Zapata, to go gack to Mr. Madero's activities.

After the resignations of the old General and Ramón Corral on May 25, that very same day the former left for the port of Veracruz from which on May 27 he sailed on the steamship Ipiranga destined to go into exile. On May 26 Francisco León de la Barra occupied the post of Provisional President, and in the north Francisco I. Madero, head of the triumphant Revolution, commenced his voyage to the capital amidst the indescribable of a people full of hope. He arrived in Mexico City on June 7. There probably has never been in the history of our country a more spontaneous crowd as this one was. Everyone wanted to greet the man who had defeated the Government of Díaz. Everyone wanted to see this man who was small of stature but a moral giant to almost all. Everyone wished to see Madero who represented the personification of the end of innumerable unjust acts, the embodiment of hope and the dream of radical change in Mexico. Don Francisco Bulnes, a prestigious writer and sharp debater, commented that the popularity of Madero in those days could be compared to that of the Virgin of Guadalupe. He was not far wrong.

Days later, Mr. Madero set up his offices at Paseo de la Reforma. Soon, a sub-rosa defamatory campaign started against him. Some newspapers, particularly a "multicolor" cartoon magazine, made a point of making vulgar criticisms and sarcastic remarks about the future president, his brother Gustavo, whom they nicknamed "ojo parado" (protruding eye, because he was cross-eyed), as well as a few of Madero's fervent followers who were secretaries of State in the Government of de la Barra. These were months of uncertainty: there seemed to be two authorities and two spheres of influence. On the one hand, the government constituted by León de la Barra, on the other Mr. Madero's moral authority, his obvious popularity and political influence; in the middle, a few dissenting groups who struggled to undermine Madero's position before he could take office. In these factions were the powerful, aristocratic and industrial groups who saw their secular privileges threatened. On the other hand, factions within the revolutionary groups were emerging; some wanted Dr. Vázquez Gómez as Vice-President, others, including Madero, wanted Pino Suárez. Problems were not resolved in a decisive manner, such as the one concerning the revolutionary forces whose leaders were dissatisfied when their divisions were disbanded; the agrarian problem, the army problem, and many others, which were solved through compromise. Attorney Federico González Garza, one of Madero's most faithful friends, wrote him letters in which he warned Madero of the dangers he perceived. With regard to the press campaign to defame Madero, he says: "We see it in the reprehensible attitude of all the newspapers of the capital, with the exception of one or two, whom it seems have forgotten that you are the savior of a nation, if we observe how they are sowing feelings of alarm and distrustfulness in the bosoms of the masses by painfully exaggerating the least significant matter and provoking hard feelings between both armies (the revolutionary and the federal); you are losing ground because you are not considered firm enough to control the many anarchistic elements whose disturbances augment day by day."

The electoral campaign went at full speed. Primary elections were held on October 1st and secondary elections on October 15th. The Constitutional Progressive Party nominated for President and Vice-President, Messrs. Madero and Pino Suárez; the Anti-reelectionist Party, Madero and Vázquez Gómez, and the Catholic Party, Madero and de la Barra. The winners of the election were Madero and Pino Suárez, who were candidates on the Constitutional Progressive Party's ticket. On November 6th Madero would occupy the presidential chair. Possibly, the man who best described these months was Don Manuel Calero, an attorney, who in his book *A Decade of Mexican Politics,* says about de la Barra's Government: "In the midst of the most lamentable political upheaval, generally incoherent and without direction, rioting everywhere, revealing the tremendous lack of discipline which was the aftermath of the Revolution, we pass into the anguished period of the Provisional Government, ever with the puerile hope that 'when the Revolution sets up its own government' —so said the venerable cliché— "the country would again reach a state of equilibrium." In the next chapter we shall study the Government of Don Francisco I. Madero.

*Venustiano Carranza. Commander-in-Chief of the Constitutionalist Army and Commissioner of Executive Power during the Revolution.*

# 3

Francisco I. Madero's regime. Problems during his regime. Zapatism. Attempted uprising of General Bernardo Reyes. The Orozco rebellion (March to July, 1912). Félix Diaz's uprising at Veracruz (October, 1912). The "Tragic Ten Days" of February 1913. Deaths of Madero and Pino Suárez. General Victoriano Huerta comes to power.

Rarely in the history of Mexico has a government begun with such good omens: a man who was very popular would come to power; everything seemed to indicate that a new era was commencing full of realities for the Mexican people, one which awakened after a lethargy of more than 30 years. Democracy would finally be a reality and not a dream. However, not everything was rose-colored: there was discontent among the revolutionaries; people were saying that Madero had not fulfilled all the promises he had made during the Revolution; that the privileged and conservative class remained untouched; that the Federal army had not been dissolved; and that, to the contrary, the revolutionary forces had been discharged. The press, supported by conservative elements, had campaigned tenaciously to undermine President Madero and some of the people close to him, like his brother Gustavo who had great influence on the President and who was nicknamed "ojo parado" (protruding eye) because of his glass eye. However, Madero who was a good and idealistic man, was sure he could lead Mexico on the path to prosperity and justice. Unfortunately, he was wrong. Adverse forces were opposed to this noble man and, through the apparent calm, low passions came to the boiling point throughout the country which would bring as a consequence the death of the Apostle of Democracy, as he has been justly called. Possibly one of his greatest defects was his unswerving optimism which did not let him see clearly the confusing situation which he had caused; he could not evaluate with a clear mind the gigantic problems of a which for 33 years had been subject to iron rule which suddenly awakened to a liberty that it did not know how to use.

Early in November, 1911, the new regime was installed. The President appointed the following persons to form his cabinet: Attorney Manuel Calero (Foreign Department); Abraham González (Department of the Interior); his uncle, Ernesto Madero (Treasury and Public Credit); General José González Salas (War and Navy Department); Manuel Vázquez Tagle (Justice); (Development and Colonization); Attorney Rafael L. Hernández (Industry);

engineer Manuel Bonilla (Communications and Public Works) and Attorney Miguel Díaz Lorbardo (Public Education).

The new regime had difficulties from the start, as mentioned in the last chapter: Zapata did not wish to recognize Madero so he proclaimed the Plan of Ayala; the press started a campaign against the government; his old supporters mistrusted him and did not look favorably on the way in which the government was progressing as they wanted more radical measures so that the revolutionary aims could be carried out. However, deaf to the outcry, Madero followed the path which he believed to be the right one. Attorney Manuel Calero, member of his cabinet and former ambassador to the United States, in his book *Un Decenio de Política Mexicana* (A Decade of Mexican Politics), describes Madero as follows:

"Madero was a liberal and a democrate and in these two ideologies, taken at face value, we were in complete accord. What we would object to, judging by his performance during the interim period, would be the procedures followed under his persidency. However, I expected them to change as he fully realized the responsibilities that came with the office of President of the Republic. It is a fact that Madero entered the government with his head full of vain formulas; that his vacilating will power was subject to violent changes and unexpected turns; that he did not know men well; that he had not studied administration; and that he had no political experience. However, in spite of these failings his heart burst with patriotism, goodness and honesty." In a broad sense, we believe that Calero's appraisal can be accepted.

Politically-speaking, one of the figures which again came to the fore in the last months of 1911 was General

Bernardo Reyes, of whom we have spoken previously. This man who was quite popular in his time, later lost the esteem of the people since he did not have sufficient courage to oppose General Díaz politically; perhaps because he had grown both politically and militarily under the long government of the Victor of April 2nd. At any rate, his popularity had waned. However, his followers made him believe that he could still become President of Mexico; but this would only be possible by using force as Madero had already been elected. One of the people greatly influencing General Reyes was his son Rodolfo who hated Madero vehemently. At the end of September, the General secretly left Mexico for the United States settling in San Antonio where his son Rodolfo soon would join him. In San Antonio, Texas, supported by a group of followers, he decided to overthrow the Mexican Government, so he started to buy arms, horses and ammunition. The United States Government became aware of these activities and arrested a goodly number of his followers, seizing arms, ammunition and other military stores. Desperate, the old general escaped to Matamoros crossing the border with a few men in December 1911. Prior to this he had published a Manifesto and Revolutionary Plan, issued at the La Soledad Ranch, State of Tamaulipas, although this document was actually drawn up in San Antonio, Texas. He had also chosen his cabinet, appointing Alfonso Mariscal y Piña as Secretary of Foreign Affairs; Manuel Garza Aldape in Immigration; Fernando Ancira in Treasury; his son Rodolfo in the Justice Department; etc.

Once in Mexican Territory, he realized that the hundreds of followers which he thought were waiting for him were only a figment of his imagination. Soon afterward the few men he did have abandoned him. Near La Parrita Ranch, leading a few faithful followers among which were Attorney David Reyes Retana, Miguel Quiroga and Santos Cavazos, he engaged in a skirmish against the forces of Colonel Ignacio Naranjo. After this brief skirmish, his few followers dispersed. That night a lone rider arrived at the rural barracks of Linares, Nuevo León, asking to speak to the commander, Lieutenant Plácido Rodríguez. Brought before him, he said "I am General Bernardo Reyes and I come to give myself up. I alone am guilty and wish to assume full responsibility in this matter. I ask that the men who followed me be pardoned. I wish nothing for myself except that I be judged by the full force of the law." He asked to get in touch with his old friend, General Jerónimo Treviño, and wrote the following message to him: "I called the army and the people to arms and there was no response. I consider this attitude to be one of protest, and I have resolved not to wage this war against the Government. I place myself in your hands." General Treviño replied by giving orders to free General Reyes in Linares under oath.

At a Council of Ministers in Mexico City, it was agreed that General Reyes be brought to the capital and tried by court-martial. This was done. General Reyes was incarcerated at Santiago Tlaltelolco, a military prison, where he was accused of insurrection. Soon afterwards, Attorney Reyes Retana and his son Rodolfo joined him. Months later his trial would take place and he would be sentenced to death. This sentence was never carried out thanks to Mr. Madero's generosity in pardoning him. The Government had come out unscathed from this First subversive attempt, one which was significant because of General Reyes' undeniable reputation in the Army. Thus it seemed that Mr. Madero had been able to elude this first difficulty. The prestigious author Don José Vasconcelos in his book *Ulysses Creole,* comments on this incident in Mr. Madero's life: "The humiliations dispensed on his enemies hurt him and he would have liked to unlock the jail gates for them and also open wide his frail arms in welcome." An admirable thought which shows the always kind attitude of the Apostle of Democracy.

However, meantime a more serious uprising was being planned in the North. Pascual Orozco, the former muleteer turned general, deeply resented Madero. He had not been appointed Governor of Chihuahua as he had wished, and he let himself be influenced by the innuendos of Chihuahua's upper class. In 1910 it was said that the State of Morelos belonged to 27 families, but the extensive northern State of Chihuahua belonged to only one: the Terrazas family who was related to the Creels, another very powerful family. These families were typical examples of political conservatism and were very rich; they began to undermine the Central Government from Chihuahua. Their first attack was against Don Abraham González, appointed Secretary of the Interior in the new government. They also attacked Orozco's rustic pride: they made him "rub elbows" with the society of Chihuahua and convinced him that he should not recognize the Federal Government.

Preparations were made, propaganda was carried out aimed at old revolutionaries, and rural forces convinced. When everything was supposedly ready, on January 26, 1911, Pascual Orozco resigned his commission as Commander of the Rural Zone. A few days later Ciudad Juárez fell to the garrison in revolt; in Chihuahua the interim government was not recognized and General Antonio Rojas, who was an active supporter of Attorney

Emilio Vázquez Gómez, was freed. The seriousness of the situation forced the Government to send Don Abraham González to Chihuahua to either reach an agreement with the rebels or, in case he was unsuccessful, fight them. The whole of March was a month of turmoil in Chihuahua: Vazquez's men occupied the State capital, the important city of Juárez, and other points of lesser importance. On March 3 Pascual Orozco revealed his true position and publicly disowned Mr. Madero, his old boss and protector. All the principal social classes of Chihuahua, the capital of the State, gave him their support since the majority of the upper classes hated and despised Governor González. At any time he wished, Orozco could count on a force of 600 men under his command and another 150 men in Casas Grandes. As was the custom, the plan in question was published, naming it the "Packing House Plan". It stated that the success of the plans of San Luis, Tacubaya and Ayala would be upheld although a few new ideas were introduced in its 37 points. The first accused Madero of selling himself to North American capital; the second referred to labor, proposing measures for changing the conditions of the working class; the third referred to the agrarian problem which, to some extent, made the demands of the Plan of Ayala more palatable. The Plan was signed by Madero's principal revolutionary leaders like José Inés Salazar, Emilio Campa, Benjamín Argumedo, Cheché Campos and others. In addition, Orozco was proclaimed Generalissimo of the Revolutionary Army. By March 8 two trains were ordered to leave Chihuahua for Juárez with the vanguard of the rebel forces.

Meantime, in Mexico City the Secretary of War resigned his post, asking the President of the Mexican Republic to

*Federal soldiers boarding a convoy. With them, the inseparable "soldadera".*

make use of his services in fighting the rebels. Mr. Madero accepted the offer and appointed him Commander of the Northern Division scheduled to combat the rebels; General Angel García Peña was appointed to fill the vacant post.

The Northern Federal Division had a force numbering about 2,150 men, organized into three brigades: An infantry and two cavalry, commanded as follows:

1. Infantry Brigade, commanded directly by General González Salas;
2. First Cavalry Brigade, commanded by Brigadier General Fernando Trucy Aubert; and
3. Second Cavalry Brigade, commanded by Brigadier General Joaquín Téllez.

Nicolás Martínez was Chief of Staff of the Division. On March 8th they left Mexico City for Chihuahua and President Madero himself saw them off at the train station.

The rebels under the command of General José Inés Salazar, numbering 3,000 in all and having four units of artillery, were stationed in the town of Jiménez. Knowing this, General González Salas marched to encounter them; the infantry left by train and the cavalry advanced on horseback. They left on March 20th from the city of Torreón. On March 24th they reached the outskirts of Jiménez where the Federal Commander was told that Government troops had skirmished with the rebel outpost. "Where are we?" asked the General, looking out of the Pullman window. "In Rellano, sir," answered an officer, "at 1,313 kilometers." "What a number!", smiled the General.

While this conversation was taking place, Orozco's men, commanded by General Emilio Campa, had loaded a locomotive with dynamite naming it the "Crazy Machine" and, taking advantage of the irregular terrain, plunged it toward the south at full speed. The writer Rafael F. Muñoz in his book, *They Took the Canyon to Bachimba,* describes the scene: "Soon afterwards a blaze of red could be seen on the vast plain in the direction taken by the locomotive, as if a piece of the sun had fallen on the tracks, followed by a tremendous explosion." In reality the locomotive had crashed into the Federal train, killing and injuring many soldiers of the 6th Battalion and a few sappers. When the explosion was heard, the troops of the 20th, 29th and 33rd Battalions as well as the Mountain Artillery Battalion disembarked and confronted Orozco's troops who, under Campa's command, occupied the hills surrounding Rellano Canyon; Rellano Station —part of the central railroad system— was located on the northern pass of this canyon.

The Federal troops could not hold back the advance of the rebels. Therefore, at 1:30 p.m. the Federal officer ordered the retreat of the infantry and the march to Torreón began an hour later. General González Salas, unable to bear the brunt of defeat, in an act of military honor, committed suicide within the Pullman car which he occupied as the train reached Bermejillo Station.

The new Commander of the Northern Division appointed by President Madero, was Brigadier General Victoriano Huerta, who had sent an escort for General Díaz when he was forced into exile and who had recently led the Federal troops fighting against Zapata in Morelos. At the request of Madero himself, Provisional President León de la Barra had relieved Huerta of his commission since it was said that he was exceedingly cruel during his campaign, General Huerta, who will become quite an important character in our story, is described by an eye witness of the time as follows:

"General Victoriano Huerta was a man of a slightly-below average height, he had a very broad back, heavy shoulders and small waist, long arms and short legs. He was a pure-blooded Huichol Indian and his features gave him away; his hair was cropped short. Everyone who laid eyes on General Huerta had an undefined impression of him."

Undoubtedly he was a personality; people felt his presence but at the same time they felt that this man lacked something, something he had lost or had never possessed. He was unfathomable like all Indians, but loquacious like few of them, and his enigmatic eyes were hidden behind thick eyeglasses, sometimes he wore bluish other times yellowish ones. A strange restlessness continually shook his powerful frame: a sudden turn of the head or a quick jerk of a hand or leg. His words were measured at times but rushed out at others, always spoken in a monotonous tone of voice. His teachers and classmates spoke of his evident talent and good schoolwork; his friends spoke of his gaiety and cheating; and the cultured men who dealt with him spoke of an incredible ignorance which suggested he had totally forgotten his schooling. However all agreed that he was rash, distrustful and suspicious.

On the other hand, the Cuban ambassador at that time, Márquez Sterling, describes him as follows: "Orozco's new opponent was born in the State of Jalisco. Having military training, he was intelligent, ambitious, quiet, astute, cold and, in short, the prototype of the Spanish-American soldier of the mid-nineteenth century."

On Friday, April 19, the new commander departed from Buenavista Station for Torreón where the greater part of the Northern Division was stationed; it had been reinforced and now had a strength of 4,800 men. This time it had within its ranks the Villa Brigade, commanded by Brigadier Francisco Villa, of the irregular army, with a total of 700 riders, which had among its leaders Tomás Urbina, the well known "compadre" (friend or comrade), Manuel Chao and Maclovio Herrera, who would all have important roles in the Revolution.

In addition, there was a powerful artillery; this service would take a decisive part in the operations. The artillery was commanded by a distinguished artilleryman, Lieutenant Colonel Guillermo Rubio Navarrete, who had at his disposal 16 75-mm. units, eight 70-mm. units and eight machine guns. Among the artillery officers was Captain Enrique Gorostieta who, as the years passed, would become Commander-in-Chief of the "Cristero" Army (1926-1929).

At the head of this new force, General Huerta engaged in battle at Conejos, Durango (May 23, 1912), where he defeated Orozco's men, who suffered heavy losses (400 dead and 200 wounded), and took considerable spoils of war. The victorious Federal troops continued their advance until they reached the fatal Rellano Station, scene of the previous defeat. Here, on May 22 and 23, 1912, Federal troops took full vengeance on the enemy, whom they defeated once more. Again Orozco's men suffered great losses (650 men and many horses). Pascual Orozco retreated to Jiménez, destroying the railroad as he went. A few days later an incident occurred which could have changed the course of the Revolution. General Huerta ordered Francisco Villa to be shot because of his ostensible insubordination: Villa refused to return a mare which had been captured. Villa was brought before a firing squad, but thanks to the combined intervention of General Emilio Madero, Lieutenant Colonel Raúl Madero (both brothers of the President) and Lieutenant Colonel Rubio Navarrete, the execution was suspended at the last moment. Huerta decided to send him to Mexico City to be court-martialed. Destiny had played a part in putting in Huerta's hands the man who would be the principal figure in his downfall. However, this is how history is written and Huerta pardoned Villa's life without stopping to consider that a year later another Northern Division, this time composed of Villa's men, would defeat him decisively. Villa at one time also had Obregón in his power and he had also wanted to have him shot, but he pardoned him. Soon afterwards, Obregón would be digging the grave of the Villa movement.

Then came the battle at La Cruz, Chihuahua (June 16, 1912), in which Orozco's men, General Rojas and General Luis Fernández, were also defeated.

On July 3rd and 4th, 1912, the conclusion of this uprising unfolded at the Canyon of Bachimba, State of Chihuahua. Here Pascual Orozco stationed himself with 6,000 men and four units of artillery and engaged in a decisive battle. This time the Federal troops completely defeated Orozco's rebels who suffered great losses in wounded and dead; a considerable booty was taken composed of prisoners and war materials. A few days later, on July 7, the Northern Division entered Chihuahua City as victors. Orozco's men led by their leader, retreated to Ciudad Juárez which was evacuated on August 20, 1912. With this retreat Orozco's rebellion was quelched, although some groups still tried to invade the State of Sonora but were unsuccessful. On July 31st of that year they still confronted the troops of Agustín Sanginés, a Federal general and the commissioned officer of the 4th Auxiliary Battalion of Sonora, commanded by Lieutenant Colonel Alvaro Obregón, an irregular soldier who will have a prominent part in the rest of this book. At that time he was 32 years' old and was: "Of regular height and weight, white, having a fine moustache, robust and jovial —and very popular. He became a soldier of sorts when some of Madero's men chided him for not taking up arms in 1910. . ."

Madero's Government had been saved and General Huerta returned to Mexico City a popular figure. Once more the President made a serious mistake: Huerta was not promoted to head a division as he hoped he would and as he well deserved. This made him hate and despise President Madero who continued governing the country with an optimism which in no way reflected the actual situation being experienced by the country. As discontent bred and disappointment spread, the conservative forces banded together so that they could overthrow Madero who, in spite of the fact that he made many mistakes, was a man of unparalleled good faith; his goodness and his passionate desire to struggle for the Mexican people no one can deny, even to sacrificing his own life. If he failed it was due to forces beyond his control, circumstances which combined to tragically end the first genuine popular and democratic government of Mexico.

On September 16, the President stood before the Congress to give his first State of Union Address. In it, among other things, he confirmed with characteristic optimism, the following:

"We hope that from now on Mexico shall enjoy an enduring peace as the principles of Effective Suffrage and

No Reelection, acquired in the Revolution of 1910, shall be the best guarantee of the functioning of Republican institutions." Poor Madero! How far he was from suspecting the terrible bloodbath which would descend on the Mexican people, many years of suffering, of hunger, of frustration, and of injustice would torment Mexico, victim of the unrestrained passions of some malevolent Mexicans. The peace hoped for and desired by the Apostle of Democracy did not delay in being newly broken by another absurd "pronouncement", this time by a singular personality, General Félix Díaz, who ironically was called "the nephew of his uncle", as he was actually the nephew of General Porfirio Díaz. Félix Díaz, upon the initiation of the Revolutionary Government, requested his retirement from the army and he retreated to the port of Veracruz where he dedicated himself to conspire against the Government. General Félix Díaz had a controversial personality, above all, because he had made his career under the aegis of his uncle and with his help. Obsessed by the glory and fame of General Porfirio Díaz, logically, he could not be in agreement with the government which had caused his uncle's downfall, and he put his efforts, his fortune and his friends to conspire against the Madero Government. Félix Díaz incorrectly assumed that the army would follow him as one, believing in a popularity which he did not possess. He chose the port of Veracruz, among other things, because in the city of Orizaba there was a garrison of the 21st Infantry Battalion under the command of his cousin Colonel José María Díaz Ordaz, and in this state Higinio Aguilar and Gaudencio González de la Llave prowled in small bands provoking uprisings. On September 16 an uprising in the port of Veracruz occurred, soon after the ex-general had arrived that dawn from Ve-

*General Emiliano Zapata, prominent figure of the Mexican Revolution.*

racruz with his relative Díaz Ordaz, the 21st Battalion, and some sections of the 39th Rural Corps. With the help of these forces they captured the military command. Félix Díaz published several proclamations: some addressed to the people of Veracruz, others to the Mexican people and to the National Army, in which he explained his attitude and justified the action he had taken. In spite of the fact that the few regular troops which garrisoned the port seconded the movement, the National Armed Units commanded by Commodore Maqueo, remained loyal to the which rapidly sent a sizable force led by General Joaquín Beltrán, to quell the rebellion. This concentration of troops was carried out rapidly and by the 21st, General Beltrán had concentrated a force of 2,000 men and ten units of artillery at Tejería Station, besides a considerable impedimenta. The force was organized in four columns which attacked Veracruz on the 33rd. The city did not resist the attack and the principal points rapidly fell into the hands of the Government forces. General Valdez, chief of one of the columns, reached the municipal palace where he obtained the rebellious general's surrender. With this brief combat, the attempt of Félix ended, thereby rapidly crumbling the absurd hopes which he might have harbored. On the 25th of that month with his principal followers, the leader of the rebellion was judged by a special court-martial and sentenced, as was to be expected, to capital punishment. A group of friends, among which was Attorney Rodolfo Reyes (son of General Bernardo Reyes), obtained suspension of sentence from the Supreme Court of Justice of the Nation, and later on, the prisoner was transferred to Mexico City. President Madero, who always avoided staining his hands with blood, commuted the death sentence. The Martyr President would pay dearly for these acts of kindness, as not many months would go by for Félix Díaz and Bernardo Reyes, who were both pardoned for grave military crimes, to become decisive factors in the fall and treacherous assassination of Madero.

On January 24, 1913, Félix Díaz arrived at the Penitentiary of Mexico City where he was immediately imprisoned. Therefore, we have in different prisons two very important participants in the drama which would unfold the following month: General Bernardo Reyes in the military prison of Santiago Tlaltelolco and in the Penitentiary the ex-general Félix Díaz. In Mexico City a group of civilian plotters and ambitious generals like Manuel Mondragón, Gregorio Ruiz, Cecilio Ocón, Rodolfo Reyes and others, were waiting for the precise moment to pounce on Madero's Government; behind the scenes the murky figure of Aureliano Blanquet lurked; and there was General Huerta full of hate and rancor toward Madero.

Unfortunately, at the end of 1912 the situation for the Government was grave: uprisings in different parts of the Republic; Emiliano Zapata up in arms in Morelos; the great oligarchic groups working intensely to undermine the Government; the ominous attitude and negative influence of the North American Ambassador Henry Lane Wilson who had an inexplicable hate for the President of the Republic, and detracting from his important post, intervened in the internal affairs of Mexico.

Attorney Manuel Calero summed up the situation correctly, as follows:

"At the end of the first year of his government, Madero was the most unpopular President of Mexico, simply because no other was the object of so little respect."

Thus we arrive at the fatal year of 1913. The month of January comes to a close rife with rumors and news that another uprising is in the offing, this time in Mexico City. The names of the people involved are bandied in whispers: General Manuel Mondragón and General Manuel Velázquez for Díaz; General Gregorio Ruiz, a deputy on behalf of Reyes; and civilians Espinosa de los Monteros, Ocón, Reyes and others who go from house to house preparing for the mutinous movement, while the generals carry out their activities in the barracks of the city. Thus the month of February arrives. During the first few days the rumors become more intense. The Government takes some precautions but, unfortunately, it does not act with the necessary expediency.

The needed financial backing for the movement was provided by a few wealthy people belonging to the so-called aristocratic circles of Mexico City like Messrs. Iñigo Noriega, Tomás Braniff, Attorney Eduardo Tamariz —a well-known member of the Catholic Party— Gabriel Fernández Somellera, Fernando de Teresa, Manuel León and others.

Everything is ready for the coup. The visible leaders, as we have mentioned before, are in military order: Brigadier General Manuel Mondragón, former chief of the Artillery Department in which he served for several years under the regime of General Díaz, who had influence among the officers of that Army and who assumed the leadership of the followers of Félix Díaz; General Gregorio Ruiz, veteran of the War of Intervention, former chief of the Cavalry Department, who also had influence among army officers, although he was a Federal deputy at that time.

On February 9 the rebellion which is known in our history as the "Tragic Ten Days", was initiated. That Sunday General Mondragón took up arms with a section of the First Cavalry Regiment (80 men) under the command of Colonel Luis G. Anaya; the rest of the corps was on military alert in Mexico City; an artillery battery of the 2nd Regiment and another of the 5th (some 80 troop men with eight 75-mm. canon), troops which were stationed in the San Diego Barracks in Tacubaya. With these numbers, he went to Santiago Tlaltelolco Prison where General Reyes was incarcerated. On the way he would pass the Liberty Barracks where a section of the Mountain Artillery would join him, and by the Mascarones Barracks where a machine gun unit would join him. However, these troops under the command of Captain Romero López and Captain Montaño went ahead to Tlaltelolco where they freed General Bernardo Reyes, one of the principal figures of the uprising.

Simultaneously, in the early hours of that fatal Sunday, the students of the Candidates' Military Academy (the school founded by General Bernardo Reyes) in the neighboring town of Tlalpan, rebelled. They went in streetcars to Mexico City led by their officers Captain Antonio Escota, Samuel H. Gutiérrez, Santiago Mendoza, de la Mora and others. Along the way Escota stopped at the San Ildefono Barracks where he incorporated a unit of the 20th Battalion which, commanded by Captain Verraza, advanced toward the National Palace while Escota continued on to the military Prison at Tlaltelolco. Having joined General Mondragón and General Ruiz, they all went to the Penitentiary of Mexico City, located on the streets of Lecumberri, where they freed General Félix Díaz. All this group began the advance toward the National Palace which they believed was in the power of the rebels. Actually, General Lauro Villar, commander of the City Garrison, had occupied the Palace with loyal forces of the 24th Battalion, relieving and detaining the students of the Candidates' School. He immediately took the following measures: he placed two machine guns in front of the main entrance of the Palace, he placed the soldiers of the 20th Battalion, lying face downward, in a line extending from the main entrance to the Mariana Entrance, and the remainder of the Palace front was covered with a unit of the 24th Battalion. Finally, at the southern portion of the Plaza, he placed 180 men of the First Cavalry Regiment. General Gregorio Ruiz advanced to the Palace believing it to be in the hands of his fellow soldiers, but he was captured there by General Villar himself. He was then taken to a stable and shot. General Ruiz died courageously requesting permission to direct the firing squad. Meanwhile, General Reyes, as he tried to march toward the Palace followed by his partisans, was killed by a machine gun blast. Attorney Rodolfo Reyes in his memoirs, describes this dramatic incident.

"In such anguished moments, positioned to the left and slightly behind my father with Dr. Espinosa de los Monteros beside him and slightly to his right, I shouted to my father: "They're killing you.'" At that same moment he swerved his mount thrusting it against a machine gun and turning toward me said: "But not in the back."

"A lone shot was heard and then all the soldiers surrounding us, in confusion, fired a terrifying and copious volley of shots, the machine guns going off at close range. My father stood still for a moment, clutching the mane of his horse, he toppled to the left falling on me who fell with the impact and found myself being dragged down by my dead mount. . ."

"Immediately after this incident, a profuse skirmish occurred which resulted in many casualties, principally among the civilians who, out of curiosity, witnessed this unusual scene."

Besides General Reyes, Colonel Morelos, commander of the 20th Battalion, died, General Villar was wounded as well as several soldiers. These rebels, upon seeing their defeat, retreated to the Citadel, a group of buildings situated on the outskirts of Belem Prison, and which was an important storehouse of arms and ammunition. In this place, in spite of the defense organized by General Manuel O. Villarreal, who died in this action, the Citadel was captured, thus falling into the hands of the rebels an important booty, as there were more than 55,000 rifles, 30,000 carbines, 100 Hotchkiss machine guns, 26,000,000 7-mm. cartridges, as well as other war supplies.

In Chapultepec Castle very early in the morning, President Madero was informed of these events. He hurriedly got up from the breakfast table and exclaimed:

"To the Palace! To the Palace! We must stir the people to action.'"

He went down to the Esplanade and ordered the cadets of the Military School to arm themselves, which they did under the orders of Lieutenant Colonel Victor Hernández Covarrubias. In this way, escorted by three units of cadets, Madero went toward the Palace where he arrived in the midst of a mob who acclaimed him. At the Palace he was received by General Villar, and the President, when he realized that the latter was wounded, ordered that he be relieved. The appointment made at that precise moment, would be the death sentence of the President as well as his brother Gustavo, who insisted on the appointment. Don Francisco was against it as he did not trust or like Huerta, but Gustavo Madero argued that since he was the leader having the highest rank among those present, he should be appointed. Due to this discussion, Mr. Madero had no choice but to give in. The transfer of command was made in the same chamber where General Villar's wounds were being dressed, and there General García Peña, Secretary of War, requested his friend Huerta to behave himself; the latter professed great loyalty which a few days later he would betray. Emphasis should be made on the designation of Huerta as this appointment would have far-reaching consequences in the history of Mexico. General García Peña, referring to the February 9th appointment, declared: "When the President gave me the order I placed my resignation in his hands, which I always carried in my pocket, and the President said to me: "I cannot believe that such a courageous man as you have today demonstrated, can leave me." I replied: "I am not abandoning you. Name me your Chief of General Staff and relieve me of the Ministerial post, which is of no account from the moment —overlooking Huerta's toast in Paso del Norte— you give him your confidence." And then he said to me: "What do you want me to do, if this is what my dear father and Gustavo want." I replied, seeing his anguish: "Well you can rot, and me too."" With this incident commenced the famous "Ten Tragic Days", which were to shatter Mexico to its very foundations, ten days of indescribable suffering of an astonished people, who did not know why they were struggling, why there was so much bloodshed, why a prompt solution was not found. President Madero saw the days go by fruitlessly, since General Huerta did not take strong measures to overthrow the

*General Francisco Villa, Commander of the
Northern Division, entering Torreón.
March, 1913.*

rebels at the Citadel. On the 11th, Huerta ordered an attack with mounted cavalry troops, rural troops of the 24th Corps, which were scattered by artillery and machine gun fire. It was said that this was a deliberate action by Huerta in order to eliminate the troops loyal to the Government. On the 13th a new attempt was made with troops of the 2nd and 7th Infantry Battalion, but this also failed. Colonel Castillo, commander of the 7th Line, lost his life in this action. The President, desperate due to the lack of action, or perhaps because he had a foreboding of treason, went to Cuernavaca to bring the prominent General Felipe Angeles, who was combating Zapata's men in the State of Morelos.

Angeles returned to Mexico City with 400 soldiers and four machine guns. All attempts against the Citadel were to no avail, cavalry attacks as well as infantry and artillery attacks failed. At last, on the 18th, President Madero and Vice-President Pino Suárez were arrested.

But let us see how treason was negotiated behind closed doors and the extent of the ominous influence of the Ambassador of the United States, Henry Lane Wilson.

"Since Saturday, the United States Embassy," so affirmed Mr. Wilson, "was the center of all activities favoring humanity." However, Mr. Márquez Sterling, Ambassador of Cuba, asserted the contrary, saying: "In all honesty, it is my understanding, now and hereafter, upon weighing the testimony of the Minister of Spain, Mr. Cologan, and the considerable evidence which time has accumulated, the Embassy was nothing but the center of a veritable intrigue against the government. Its policy before the rebellion, and especially at the present time, the policy of false information and false alarms, to which the creoles are prone and which splendidly supported the views of the disorderly Ambassador. . ." That same day a meeting was held at the Embassy where the ministers of Germany, England and Spain met and were received by a pale, nervous and excited Wilson who told them: "Madero is crazy, a lunatic and a fool and should legally be declared mentally unbalanced and unfit for the exercise of his office." And, revealing his aims and the plot in which he was so deeply involved, added: "This situation has become intolerable. . . and I shall restore order." "Four thousand men are on the way and they shall come up here if necessary." Here was the menace of foreign intervention which so many times had wielded its power against weak countries, but it produced the desired effect. On the 18th a few senators appeared at Madero's house to ask for his resignation, but the president became indignant and refused, showing them a telegram from President Taft which said: "As a consequence, your Excellency shall be warned that the information which has reached you in regard that orders have already been given to disembark troops, is not precise. . ." This put an end to Wilson's machinations, but Huerta continued working and ordered that the 29th Infantry Battalion be concentrated in Mexico City, which, under the command of his faithful friend, Brigadier General Aureliano Blanquet, was in Toluca. The unit was transferred to the capital and was stationed in the National Palace itself. Slowly but surely the vulnerable President was falling into the trap.

In the morning of the 18th, Huerta decided to unmask and ordered his subordinate and accomplice to capture the President; Blanquet sent the second commander of the Battalion, Lieutenant Colonel Jiménez Riveroll, with a group of soldiers; they entered the offices where the President was to be found. A skirmish developed on the top floor of the Palace when the soldiers tried to arrest the Chief Executive. His aides, Captain Montes and Captain Garmendia, opened fire on the captors, killing Lieutenant Colonel Riveroll and wounding Major Izquierdo. They in turn were able to shoot and kill Marcos Hernández, an engineer and cousin of Mr. Madero. However, in the confusion, the President was able to escape, hurriedly going down to the patio of the Palace. A short time before, General Blanquet had detained Vice-President Pino Suárez. Madero tried to get to the door when Blanquet reached him and, putting a hand on his shoulder, told him that he was his prisoner. Madero turned around, enraged, and managed to free himself, although Blanquet was a tall, hefty man. Once disengaged, Madero gave Blanquet a slap. However, there were many soldiers from the 29th Battalion. Huerta's Chief-of-Staff was also there, and all of them went to the aid of Blanquet, detaining the President whom they took a prisoner to a small room known as the administration office of the Palace. The treachery had been completed. The first democratic government of Mexico was overthrown with treason and bloodshed. But where was the author of this action which covered Mexico with shame? He was at a fashionable restaurant "El Gambrinus" with Gustavo, the President's brother. When Huerta was told that everything had come to an end, he quickly left the restaurant, leaving Gustavo Madero by himself. Shortly after Gustavo would also be arrested. Huerta reached the Palace about 3:00 p.m. and went straight off to see Mr. Madero, the following dialogue taking place:

"Mr. President. . ." the traitor started to say, but Mr. Madero interrupted him firmly: "Ah, so I am still President. . .?" Huerta tried to go on with his speech, and said: "From the Battle of Bachimba. . ." Madero again interrupted him: "You were already a traitor." At this the pretorian became silent and then declared: "I'm going, I just came to say hello to my prisoners." Mr. Madero then turned his back on him and, coldly replying "no!", ignored his greetings.

Thus ended this very sad incident in our history. However, we still must see the farce which was enacted that evening at the United States Embassy. In effect, that night Félix Díaz, Mondragón, Rodolfo Reyes, Fidencio Hernández, Enrique Zepeda, Huerta, Joaquín Maass and the Ambassador himself, who directed the show, gathered together at the Embassy. There was much discussion, bogus favors were granted, well paid government posts assigned, and at last at 9:00 p.m. the Plan of the Citadel, as the document was named by the rebels, was published; however, Attorney Ramón Prida in his book *From Dictatorship to Anarchy* justly called the document the Embassy Pact. Said document, prepared at the diplomatic headquarters of Lane Wilson, stated:

"In Mexico City, at nine thirty on the evening of the eighteenth of February nineteen thirteen, a meeting was held which included General Félix Díaz and General Victoriano Huerta, the former being counseled by Attornéys Fidencio Hernández and Rodolfo Reyes, and the latter by Lieutenant Colonel Joaquín Maass and Engineer Enrique Zepeda. Át such meeting General Huerta declared that because the situation of Mr. Madero's Government is untenable, in order to avoid further bloodshed and due to sentiments of national fraternity, he has imprisoned said gentleman, his Cabinet and some other persons; that he wishes to express to General Díaz his good wishes so that all the parties represented by him may fraternize, and all join to put an end to the present harrowing situation.

General Díaz declared that his movement's sole object was to obtain the good of the Nation and, therefore, he is ready for any sacrifice which will result in benefit of the country."

"After the above discussions, the aforementioned was agreed upon by those present, as follows:

"First. As of this moment the Executive Power which had been functioning, is declared null and void. The parties represented by General Díaz and General Huerta commit themselves to prevent by all means any attempt to reestablish said power."

"Second: At the earliest possible moment, we shall try to resolve, by means of the best possible legal terms, the existing situation and, General Díaz and General Huerta shall strive so that the latter may assume, before seventy-two hours have elapsed, the Provisional Presidency of the Republic, with the following Cabinet: in Foreign Affairs, Attorney Francisco León de la Barra; in the Treasury, Attorney Toribio Esquivel Obregón; in War, General Manuel Mondragón; in Development, Engineer Alberto Robles Gil; in Immigration, Engineer Alberto García Granados; in Justice, Attorney Rodolfo Reyes; in Public Instruction, Attorney Jorge Vera Estañol; in Communications, Engineer David de la Fuente."

"A new ministry shall be created which will be in charge of solving agrarian problems; this entity shall be named the Ministry of Agriculture and the offices shall be in charge of Attorney Manuel Garza Aldape."

"Third: As soon as the local situation is resolved, General Huerta and General Díaz shall be put in charge of all parties and authorities of whatever kind whose exercise is required as a guarantee."

"Fourth: General Díaz declines the offer to form part of the provisional Cabinet in case General Huerta assumes the Provisional Presidency, so that he may be free to start work with regard to the commitment he has with his Party for the next elections; he wishes to express this purpose clearly and the signers should clearly understand this."

"Fifth: The official notification to the foreign representatives shall be made immediately, limiting said notice to express the fact that the Executive Power has ceased, that a legal substitution is being provided, that meanwhile General Díaz and General Huerta are invested with full authority regarding said power, and that all guarantees corresponding to the respective citizens shall be granted."

"Sixth: Of course, we shall invite all revolutionaries to lay down their arms, in order to achieve the relative arrangements."

"Signed: General Victoriano Huerta. General Félix Díaz."

With this very important document, the betrayal of Huerta was officially culminated, upon joining the rebels of the Citadel.

A few hours after this shameful pact was signed, atrocious executions took place at the Citadel. Don Gustavo was bloodily mangled to death by a mob crazed by hate, and Don Adolfo Bassó, ex-Administrador of the Palace, was shot; he was accused of firing a machine gun on the 9th.

The following day, Huerta sent a telegram which would become a historical document, for reasons. In it he said: "Authorized by the Senate, I have assumed the executive power, the President and his Cabinet being jailed." This telegram woul have great repercussions in Coahuila and Sonora, where the Constitutional Revolutions would be born, thus ending the spurious power of Huerta.

That same day, Madero's and Pino Suárez's resignations were obtained; the former wrote his in pencil and it said: "Citizen Secretaries of the Honorable Chamber of Deputies: In view of the events which have developed in the Nation from yesterday to this moment and for a greater tranquility of same, we formally resign our duties as President and Vice-President, respectively, for which we were elected. We do so declare. Mexico, February 19, 1913. Francisco I. Madero. José M. Pino Suárez. Signatures." The resignations were sent immediately to the Chamber of Deputies who accepted them. Attorney Pedro Lascurain, who was Minister of Foreign Affairs, was named Provisional President; he lasted only 45 minutes in office, enough time to name General Huerta Secretary of the Interior and immediately resign so that the latter could be invested in the office of Provisional President of Mexico.

Meantime the illustrious prisoners were still in the small room of the Administration office of the Palace; General Felipe Angeles had joined them in prison. At that very moment, Mr. Márquez Sterling was making a great effort to save the lives of the ex-functionaries. This noble diplomat, whose attitude contrasted greatly with that of Lane Wilson, requested a warship, the cruiser Cuba, from his country, so that Madero and Pino Suárez might be put on board with their families. The families were also struggling to save their lives. Mrs. Sara P. Madero went to Ambassador Lane Wilson, and told him:

"I want you to use your influence to save the lives of my husband and of the other prisoners." Lane Wilson looked steadily at Doña Sara. P. Madero as she begged, and replied: "This is a responsibility which I cannot assume, neither in my name nor that of my government." and he added almost in a whisper: "Your husband did not

*The then-Colonel, Alvaro Obregón,
Commander of the 41st Batallion of
irregulars from Sonora, accompanied
by two of his officers.*

know how to govern. He never asked for or wanted to take my advice."

The days went by for the anguished prisioners and their families. Finally the 22nd arrived. That night at 10:00 Colonel Joaquín Chicarro and Rural Mayor Francisco Cárdenas appeared in the room which served as a prison, and said:

"Gentlemen, get up." "Where are we going?" asked Madero, standing up, surprised. "We are taking you outside. . . to the Penitentiary," replied Cárdenas. Madero and Pino Suárez hurried to comply with the order; they said goodbye to General Angeles and went outside where two black cars awaited them. Madero was escorted by Cárdenas and Pino Suárez by Rural Private Pimienta. The cars drove toward the Penitentiary. When they reached the fields belonging to the Marksmanship Academy, a holdup was feigned in which a group of the ex- officials' followers ostensibly wanted to free them —then the captors made them get out of the cars. At the precise moment in which Madero was being forced out of the car by Cárdenas, the latter whipped his gun out and shot Madero in the nape of the neck, killing him instantly.

Meantime, another drama was unfolding in the car occupied by Pino Suárez. The ex-Vice President realized that he would be assassinated. He therefore started to run, but Pimienta fired a shot which got him. The unfortunate Pino Suárez fell to the ground. To make sure he was dead, Cárdenas and Pimienta shot him several times more. It was 11:30 on the night of February 22nd —Madero and Pino Suárez had died physically. However, they both were reborn in the immortality of Mexican History since, with their lives, they pointed out to all Mexicans the way to democracy and social justice.

Years later Francisco Cárdenas would commit suicide in Guatemala City as he was being detained at the petition of the Mexican Government for his extradition. Pimienta, who ascended to the rank of general, was shot for reasons other than the crime which he had committed.

This is how General Huerta reached office, inaugurating a government which would last only until August of the following year.

# 4

The Constitutionalist Revolution. Venustiano Carranza disavows Huerta. February 19, 1913. The Plan of Guadalupe. Initial revolutionary operations. Alvaro Obregón in Sonora. Francisco Villa in Chihuahua. The Zapata movement.

We should remember that on February 18th, General Huerta sent a circular-telegram to all the Governors which declared: "With the authorization of the Senate, I have assumed Executive Power because the President and his cabinet have been imprisoned." This message was received in every State Capital of the Republic and all the Governors, with the exception of one, accepted it, including those who were revolutionaries and supporters of Madero, such as Doctor Rafael Cepeda of San Luis Potosí, Miguel Silva of Michoacán and Attorney Manuel Mestre Gigliazza of Tabasco. The lone exception was Mr. Venustiano Carranza who rejected it. The following day, February 19th, he addressed the State Congress declaring: "Since the Senate does not have authority to designate the Chief Magistrate of the nation, it cannot legally authorize General Victoriano Huerta to assume Executive Power. Therefore, the aforementioned General has not been invested legitimately as President of the Republic".

On that same date, the Congress in Coahuila, published a historical decree for various reasons; in the first place, in said decree General Huerta was disavowed as Provisional President of the Republic. Secondly, the Chief Executive of the State (Carranza) was authorized to organize military forces; in other words, this was the decree which created the present Mexican army. Because this document was basic in the history of the Revolution, we reproduce it below:

"VENUSTIANO CARRANZA, Constitutional Governor of the Free and Sovereign State of Coahuila de Zaragoza, makes known to its inhabitants that the Congress of this State has decreed the following:

"The Twelfth Constitutional Congress of the free, independent and sovereign State of Coahuila decrees: Number 1495.

"Article First. General Victoriano Huerta is disavowed in his legal capacity as Chief Executive of the Republic, which he states was conferred upon him by the Senate, and all acts and ordinances dictated by him in this capacity are also disavowed.

"Article Second. The Chief Executive of the State is granted extraordinary authority in all branches of Public Administration so that he may abolish those which he may deem pertinent and proceed to put into operation armed forces to assist in maintaining constitutional order in the Republic.

"Economic Clause. Urge all other State Governments and Commanders of Federal, Auxiliary and Rural forces of the Federation to support the decision of the Government of this State.

"DECREED this nineteenth day of February nineteen hundred and thirteen in the Chamber of Sessions of the Honorable State Congress. A. Barrera (signature), Gabriel Calzada (signature), Sánchez Herrera (signature). The above decree should be printed, communicated and observed.

Saltillo, February 19, 1913."

Mr. Carranza, before adopting this decision, met with a group of people in his own home as is mentioned by Attorney Manuel Aguirre Berlanga, in his book *Legal Origin of the Constitutionalist Revolution,* in which he states: "On that same day he met at his home with various local deputies, among them Lieutenant Colonel of the Federal Army, E. M. Luis G. Garfias and First Technical Artillery Captain, Jacinto B. Treviño, who served on Madero's Military Staff, both of whom were in Saltillo with orders to organize the irregular troops of the State. Also present were other trust-worthy people. At that meeting he declared that in his opinion "The Senate lacked constitutional authority to designate the President of the Republic, substitute the candidate who had been elected by popular vote, or authorize anyone to arrest the Chief Magistates of the Nation, and that therefore it was an unavoidable obligation of the Government of Coahuila to disavow and immediately reject such acts. Therefore if it were necessary to recur to the unusual expedient of taking up arms and bringing about a war more bloody than the Three Years'

War to restore legitimate order, the seriousness of such a circumstance should not terrify any citizen who loves his country."

Let us now see what forcés were available to Mr. Carranza on February 19th to initiate the struggle against General Huerta's army:

Lieut. Colonel Francisco Coss, of the irregular forces, who was in Saltillo with a troop which numbered 30 men; Lieut. Colonel of the Military Army, E. Luis G. Garfias with the 25th Auxiliary Regiment of the Federation (in organization( with 200 men at its disposal; Lieut. Colonel Jesús Carranza, also with the irregular forces as was his brother who was stationed in Torreón with 60 men in his troop and which was assigned to the 11th Military Zone:

and a few scattered irregular State forces located along the Saltillo-Piedras Negras railroad tracks commanded by colonel Alberto Guajardo of the irregular forces and which were headquartered in the city of Múzquiz.

In total, there were 500 mounted men, in addition to the possible reinforcement of Lieutenant Colonel Pablo González, also of the irregular forces, who were stationed in Julimes, Chihuahua, with the auxiliary Regiment "Carbineers of Coahuila."

The Federal troops who could act against M. Carranza were: those belonging to the Third Military Zone (General J. M. Miert) at the General Barracks in Monterrey, Nuevo León, some 3,000 men, scattered over a vast area, which included the States of Nuevo León and Tamaulipas, and those of the Eleventh Military Zone (Brigadier General Fernando Trucy Aubert) headquartered in Torreón, who had available some 2,000 men.

While Governor Carranza in Coahuila adopted a firm rebellious attitude, with the support of the above-mentioned leaders, let us see what was happening in other parts of the Republic.

In Chihuahua, General Pascual Orozco joined the Huerta movement. This was a strange posture for the ex-muleteer who was perhaps motivated by his memories of the defeats inflicted upon him by Huerta several months before, or even because he had greater faith in the Huerta government.

However, in the State of Coahuila outbreaks of discontented guerrillas began to appear: Manuel Chao and Tomás Urbina in the south, the brothers Luis and Maclovio. Herrera and Rosalío Hernández in the central area and Toribio Ortega, Melchor Vela and Juan Amaya in the northeast. Also among the rebellious forces in the central area was the legendary Francisco Villa, who initiated his guerrilla activities with a small group of followers who would become, a short time later, the Villa Brigade and later be known as the famous "División del Norte" (the Northern Division). Abraham González, the Madero follower who governed the area, also refused to acknowledge the new regime, but he was captured by General Antonio Rábago, Federal Commander of the State. He was sent to Mexico, but before leaving the outskirts of Chihuahua, he was assassinated, thus dying a simple man, incorruptible in his political convictions.

In Sonora, the Governor of the State, José M. Maytorena, adopted a nebulous position and did not take an open stand as to disavowing Huerta's Government, in spite of the pressures brought to bear on him by Colonels of the Federal forces such as Benjamin Hill, Alvaro Obregón and

*A group of Federal Officers at the turn of the century, in an armaments class.*

Juan G. Cabral. Finally, he decided to request sick-leave and departed, heading for the United States. The local government replaced him with Mr. Ignacio Pesqueira, who was a local deputy. The new Governor convened the local Congress on March 3rd, and on March 4th it was decided to disavow the government which had assumed power as a result of the February take-over.

The result of the above was that the important State of Sonora was now inclined to support the Revolutionary movement and some of the leaders who later were to hold high-ranking positions in the history of Modern Mexico, rapidly initiated military operations. Among these were Lieutenant Colonel Plutarco Elías Calles, Colonel Salvador Alvarado, Captain Abelardo Rodríguez and, of course, in a prominent place, General Alvaro Obregón. The Sonora forces were composed of some 4,000 men (3,300 in infantry and 700 in cavalry). Armed with the regulations Mauser rifle and the 30-30 carbines, the greater part of these armed forces lacked real military training, although they were under the command of leaders and officers who did have war experience as they had had combat experience in the Madero revolution and, in addition, some of them had participated in the Orozco campaign.

The Federal forces had at their command some 5,500 men (2,100 line troops, 1,600 federal auxiliaries and 1,800 irregulars, with little or no discipline). These forces were part of the First Military Zone commanded by Brigadier General Miguel Gil with General Headquarters at Torin, Sonora.

There were other outbreaks throughout the Republic, but not as important. In Nuevo León Francisco Murguía and Antonio Villarreal began to operate; in the southern part of Coahuila and Zacatecas the brothers Luis and Eulalio Gutiérrez and Pánfilo Natera; in Michoacan Gertrudis Sánchez, Joaquín Amaro and Héctor F. López took up arms; in San Luis Potosí the brothers Carrera Torres and the brothers Cedillo joined the uprising; in Sinaloa, Juan Carrasco and Ramón F. Iturbe; in Guerrero the brothers Figueroa; in Tabasco, Segovia, Greene and others.

The Revolution spread uncontainably all over the Republic, and we should not forget that Zapata continued in his rebellious attitude with more reason than ever now that he saw his old enemies elevated to power because, in addition to Huerta, also in power was the ferocious Aureliano Blanquet who had caused so much damage to the followers of Zapata with his 29th Batallion.

Let us return now to Carranza who was the one who raised the flag of legality and, in conjunction with the Plan of Guadalupe, published in the Hacienda of the same name, gave political as well as military meaning to the new movement. Let us see how an eye-witness who took part in the events at that time, describes this momentous incident. We refer to General Francisco J. Múgica who years later participated outstandingly in national affairs and was the instigator of the idea of the petroleum expropriation which took place in 1936. In Armando de María y Campos' book *Autobiographical Chronicle,* he declares as follows:

"From that frustrating and fatal afternoon —writes Múgica— forced marches through immense and penurious thistle-impregnated steppes, divested of any oasis became the order of the day. . ."

"But on the 25th we arrived at the Hacienda of Guadalupe located strategically in a solitary valley which begins in the fertile glens of Boca de Tres Ríos. The hacienda afforded us the strategic security of the nearby ranges of mountains; the refreshment of the scarce but much appreciated waters from its streams, relief of the physical exhaustion of the men and the horses who had barely eaten and rested in the bare fields for short periods of time, only to take up the march again, and lastly it afforded them the shelter of the hacienda's trojes (granaries) and sheds for the horses, evoking memories of happier days.

"Once they had bathed, their battered nerves soothed by their new surroundings, Carranza, their leader, and his private secretary, Captain Breceda, closeted themselves in the Payroll Office of the ranch. All of us anticipated some welcome news. Conjectures were made that a new march would shortly be announced, or that a new and more pleasing campaign project was being planned. But this was not the case; the private meeting of the governor, Don Venus, the nickname given him by the crude border men, was prolonged and, as always, serious in tone, ending with the imperious blast of the General Barrack's trumpet summoning the commanders and officers.

"Evoking memories from the panorama of the past, I recall the presence of officers and commanders of the Second group of Carabineers from Coahuila under the command of the modest and guileless Lieut. Colonel Cesareo Castro; the officers and commanders of the First Regiment, "Free Men of the North", led by the elegant and attractive Lieut. Colonel Lucio Blanco; a few men who remained from the shattered and crushed Second Regiment, Carabineers of San Luis, whose leader, Lieut. Colonel Andrés Saucedo was ill in Monclova; a few officers who served in the 28th Federal Regiment, which was then in organization, having joined our ranks and files almost intact, commanded by its leader, Lieut. Col. Luis Garfias. Also present were a small number of modest officers who served as escort to the Commander-in-Chief. These men, commanded by Major Aldo Baroni and the humble but brave Captain Gaspar Cantú, were always at their posts in times of danger and strife. Also in the group were the indomitable officers and the heroic leader of the Second Corps of the "Free Men of the North" commanded by the somber, curt and bizarre Lieut. Colonel Francisco Sánchez Herrera; also the never-to-be-forgotten men who had fallen in action: Agustín Millán, Antonio Portas and the enthusiastic group from Veracruz with the rural regiments under their command and lastly, the young assistants, who, under the orders of the Head of the Military Staff, Lieut. Colonel Jacinto B. Treviño, were ever anxious for new adventures and for the social channeling of the Revolution."

"All of them in good spirits, happy and steadfast filed into the small room in which hours before Carranza and his private secretary had closeted themselves. It was a tiny, quadrangular room, with a small window in the center of the wall facing the camp and a narrow door which gave access to a sort of vestibule of medium-size with sheds where shoeing, carpentry shops and rudimentary farm implements were kept. Two dirty, termite-eaten tables and two chairs were the sole furnishings of that office in which the above-mentioned officers in a column of less than 700 men were to ratify a pact with the Constitutional Government of Coahuila and the entire nation to defend and bring the revolutionary plan to ultimate triumph. Due to one of those mysterious and unknown circumstances of destiny the plan would henceforth be known as the "Plan of Guadalupe."

This plan contained a Manifesto to the Nation and consisted in effect of seven important points in which General Huerta was disavowed as President, as was the legislative and judicial bodies of the Federation. Also disavowed were the governments of those states which had acknowledged Huerta's regime. It was established that the new army would be known as "Constitutionalist" and Carranza adopted the title of Commander-in-Chief, not accepting any military rank; in other words, from the first Carranza desired his movement to be endowed with civilian characteristics. It was also established that upon the triumph of the Revolution, elections for President of the Republic would be convoked.

The Revolution began to extend principally in the northern part of the country. Nevertheless, Carranza was unfortunate in his first military operations. For this reason he decided to go to Sonora where the revolutionaries, headed by the brilliant Obregón, were obtaining resplendent victories against the federal garrisons.

Upon leaving Coahuila, some of his followers headed for different parts of the Republic. One of these was Lucio Blanco who went north to Matamoros, Tamaulipas which was near the United States border. In a nearby place, in the Hacienda de Borregos, the owner of which was General Félix Díaz, a historic event of great importance took place: social, not military. There the first distribution of land was undertaken. In this apportionment the then Captain Francisco J. Múgica participated. It was his idea to divide the vast ranch. After the assignment of lands was accomplished, on August 29th the first land deeds were issued. Jean Jaures, the noted French socialist leader, upon learning of the distribution of lands in Matamoros, exclaimed: "Now I realize what the fight in Mexico is about". This act apparently did not have the complete approval of the Commander-in-Chief, as Mr. Carranza reprehended Lucio

Blanco and ordered his transfer to the State of Sonora, where he remained under orders to General Obregón.

Meanwhile, Carranza, after staying in various places in Coahuila, and his defeat in Torreón, decided to go to Durango where the brothers Arrieta had proclaimed themselves in his favor. From Coahuila he travelled to the zone of operations in the northwest controlled by Obregón, and initiated his march to El Fuerte, Sinaloa, a site which had been overtaken by the victorious Sonora forces.

On September 20th he arrived at El Fuerte where he was greeted with all honors by General Alvaro Obregón and, accompanied by the latter, he went to the capital of Sonora, the city of Hermosillo, where he was welcomed most enthusiastically.

Let us regress a few months, to review, although briefly, the military campaign of General Alvaro Obregón in Sonora.

For the better understanding of the reader, we shall divide the operations in two: those in the northern part of Sonora and those which took place in the southern part of the State. The first phase, that which took place in the northern area, took Obregón 40 days, at the end of which he had wiped out the enemy from that important area of the State and with which he also secured the border with the United States through which he could export cattle, and import arms and ammunition so necessary to the cause of the revolutionaries.

The principal operations were the capture of the important border city of Nogales; later the acquisition of Cananea's mineral resources, the value of which was considerable; the battles waged in the city of Naco and the subsequent occupation of that city (March 26th to April 13, 1913). The capture of Naco culminated in the flight of General Ojeda with part of his garrison to the United States, from which they were repatriated to Mexico. General Ojeda, in spite of his defeat in Naco, received orders from General Huerta to take charge of the Yaqui Division (División del Yaqui) which was located in the southern part of the State of Sonora.

In the southern part of the State, the principal battles were those in Santa Rosa (May 9-11, 1913), the maneuvers at Estación Ortiz and the battle of Santa María (June 19-26, 1913) and also the siege of the port of Guaymas (June 27-July 13, 1913). It must be noted that this city did not fall into the hands of the revolutionaries and that it remained besieged during the rest of the civil war up to about the middle of the following year.

Subsequent to these operations which practically gave Obregón control of the entire State, he proceeded southward, fighting in the State of Sinaloa where, as we have seen, he had his first meeting with Commander-in-Chief, Carranza.

Let us go now to the State of Chihuahua where the famous Francisco Villa operated. In the southern part of the State, Commanders Chao and Luis as also Maclovio Herrera lay siege to the city of Parral, defended by the federal forces. Meanwhile, in the northern and central part of the State, Pancho Villa initiated his brilliant career.

In the meantime Mr. Carranza made important political and military decisions. In El Fuerte he appointed General Obregón Commander of the Northeastern Army and designated his first revolutionary cabinet, putting Attorney Rafael Zubarán in charge of the Department of the Interior and Mr. Adolfo de la Huerta (a future President of Mexico) as Chief Clerk. He ratified the appointment of Attorney Francisco Escudero, Undersecretary of State; Gen-

*A peasant, turned revolutionary, opens fire on the "federals".*

eral Felipe Angeles, a distinguished artilleryman, an ex-federalist who had joined the revolutionary movement in Sonora, having come from the United States where he had immigrated from France, was put in charge of the Department of State. As Chief Officers of the Communications and Development Secretaryships respectively, he named Engineer Ignacio Bonillas and his private secretary, Attorney Gustavo Espinosa Mireles. Of these appointments the one which caused the most changes and problems was that of General Angeles because the revolutionaries did not look kindly on the appointment of a general with federalist leanings as Undersecretary of War. They did not accept an upstart, as he was called, holding an executive post in the Government. This, among other things, was the beginning of the break between Angeles and Carranza, a falling out that would cause the budding revolution innumerable problems.

In the city of Hermosillo, where Mr. Carranza had arrived, as stated above, the Commander-in-Chief delivered a most important speech in which his social ideology, which later would be incorporated in other official documents of the Revolution, was made evident. On that occasion, he stated, among other things:

"The time has come to cease making false promises to the people so that at least one man can go down in history who does not mislead them or offer them the moon and the stars, doubly offending the Mexican people by judging that they require flattering promises to prepare themselves for the armed struggle in defense of their rights. For this reason, gentlemen, the Plan of Guadalupe does not imply a utopia or anything which is unattainable, or ill-conceived promises with no real intention of complying with them. The Plan of Guadalupe is a patriotic appeal to all social classes, not a supply and demand type operation with the proceeds going to the highest bidder. However, the Mexican people should realize that once the armed struggle called for in the Plan of Guadalupe is at an end, the formidable and majestic social struggle must begin: the class struggle, whether we want it or not, no matter who opposes it, and the new social concepts will have to be imposed on our people. We are not only referring to the distribution of lands and natural resources, or to free elections and the establishment of new schools. This is something much greater and sacred; it is the establishment of justice, the seeking of equality, the disappearance of the mighty, in order to establish equilibrium in the national economy."

"The people have lived fictitiously, hungry and miserable, with a fistful of laws which in no wise favor them. Everything will have to be changed. A new constitution must be created, the beneficial action through which no once can deprive the people.

"We lack laws which favor the tillers of the soil and the laborers, but they will be the ones who will promulgate them because they are the ones who will triumph in this struggle for repossession and social justice.

"The reforms which have been stated and which are beginning to be put into practice as the Revolution advances southward, shall bring about a total change in everything and shall open up a new era for the Republic."

Meanwhile, in the south, in Morelos, Zapata continued his ceaseless struggle against the Huerta doctrine. The new governor was General Juvencio Robles, hated passionately by the majority of the people of Morelia and his designation increased the rancor and revived the struggle. General Robles put into effect draconian measures, clustering the families of the rebels in veritable concentration camps which resulted in the near disintegration of most of the smaller towns and rural communities.

Zapata was forced to modify some of the tenets of the Plan of Ayala. Also new measures were taken to regulate commander and officer relations in the Zapata troops, necessitating payment of some kind of salary to the poor southern farmers.

The arbitrary measures taken by Robles had their results, but they were negative for the Governor because the revolution began to spread extensively, and the Zapata forces again began to threaten the suburbs of Mexico City, gaining access to Milpa Alta, Tlalpan and other points to the south of the capital. These unpopular measures gave rise to Huerta's decision to definitely relieve Juvencio Robles of his duties, replacing him with Brigadier General Adolfo Jiménez Castro, who had already served in Morelos the year before under the command of General Angeles.

The performance of General Jiménez Castro was different; the greater part of the people were able to live more comfortably and the federal garrisons acted more as a police service than an occupation troop. This had the effect of making the federal forces virtual rulers of the cities, while the Zapata forces were in control of the fields, although the latter were desolate and abandoned as a result of the civil war. These new tactics forced Zapata to leave the State and transfer his base of operations to the neighboring State of Guerrero.

Obviously the successful results obtained by the revolutionaries in the north were reflected in the south, renewing the fervor of the Zapata followers. Troops were diverted to the north, thus alleviating the situation in Morelos, Guerrero and the State of Mexico. Nevertheless Zapata continued to be plagued with an endemic shortage of arms and ammunition and this led to limited action in these regions, operations being reduced to guerrilla warfare in Morelos, Guerrero, Puebla, the State of Mexico and certain areas in proximity with the Federal District.

# 5

The Victoriano Huerta Government. The great battles of the Revolution. The Tampico incident. The occupation of Veracruz. The Niagara Falls Conferences. Revolutionary victories. Surrender and dissolution of the Federal Army. August 1914. Resignation of Huerta. Occupation of the Capital of the Republic by the triumphant Revolutionaries.

The Government of General Huerta could not initiate its work under good auspices. The murders of Madero and Pino Suárez were indelible stains on his government which had emerged from the coup and from hateful compromises which had culminated in the infamous Pact of the Embassy. Huerta's attitude was never sincere and he soon maneuvered to neutralize one of his partners, General Félix Díaz, by offering him the post of ambassador to Japan, by way of thanks for sending the Japanese mission during the Centennial festivities. The Japanese Government, aware of aware of the situation, discreetly made excuses for not welcoming General Díaz, saying that the royal family would not be in Tokyo until several months later. Another political step taken by Huerta was the indefinite postponement of elections, which violated the pact. These measures resulted in a ministerial crisis in which the ministers who were partial to Félix Díaz resigned, among them Engineer Alberto García Granados, who held the cabinet post of the Interior Toribio Esquivel Obregón, of Public Education Manuel Mondragón, who had become the scapegoat for the military defeats suffered by the federal forces and who was forced to relinquish his post to General Aureliano Blanquet because of an irrefutable order given by Huerta. Mondragón was banished into exile. A trip as a member of an investigating committee abroad was the excuse given for his departure. Attorney Rodolfo Reyes also resigned.

Obviously, discontented people appeared in Mexico City itself, or else people whom Huerta could not trust because of their affiliations with Madero. The first to fall was General Gabriel Hernández, a revolutionary leader from Hidalgo, who was imprisoned at the Belem Jail. At dawn of March 23 he was taken out of his cell by orders of Engineer Enrique Cepeda, Governor of the Federal District, and shot in the prison yard. Then his body was incinerated. The case provoked great speculation and Engineer Cepeda was discharged from his post and tried. However, it was alleged that the murderer had been mentally disturbed when he had ordered the shooting of Hernández. Months later Engineer Cepeda disappeared without anyone knowing for certain his whereabouts or if he had died.

The Chamber of Deputies, influenced by the Huerta coterie, decided to postpone elections for President and Vice-President. As we have said before, this increased the differences already evident among the captors of the Citadel, and, as a consequence, on April 24, 1913, the candidates, General Félix Díaz and Francisco León de la Barra, resigned their respective nominations. Consequently, they sent a letter to Attorney José Luis Requena, President of their party. In this letter Félix Díaz gives the reasons for his resignation. Among other things, he says:

"To prolong this fratricidal struggle because the convocation has not been issued or is being postponed indefinitely, would be like denying the story of my life and staining it; as a citizen I have worshiped duty and as a soldier, honor, perhaps an inexplicable inconsistency, but as far as I am concerned, I do not intend to dishonor my past or my future."

"According to the Chamber's vote, peace in the Republic does not depend on immediate elections, as you and I believe: judging from those who have upheld this hallowed thesis, it is doubtful, to say the least, that they (the elections) will contribute to attaining peace; therefore, our duty lies in abstaining from taking any action contrary to this resolution, relinquishing the responsibility to the party having the legal and historical obligation."

Another letter, written in similar terms by Attorney Francisco León de la Barra, was addressed to Attorney Requena, President of the Liberal Democractic Party.

There were also worthy men in Congress who were opposed to the new state of affairs. Among those who

*A group of pro-Zapata
soldiers in operation in Morelos State.*

paid with their lives for their manliness, were Deputy Edmundo Pastelín, murdered on June 13, Deputy Adolfo G. Gurrión, murdered August 17 and Deputy Serapio Rendón, murdered on August 22. Rendón was an influential member of the parliamentary groups known as reformers. Huerta had tried to win him over, but Rendón refused, saying: "That he could in no way betray his companions or renounce the principles which he had professed to all his life. . ."

As a consequence of this unwavering position, his murder was planned in the town of Tlalnepantla and committed there in a small room of a municipal building. He was shot to death, and a few days later his body was taken to a modest cemetary called "La Loma" (the Hill) near Tlalnepantla.

Before he died, Deputy Rendón tried to write a letter to his family. The first line still exists and reads: "Adorable wife, ido. . ." It seems he was about to write "idolized children" when his life was cut short with a bullet in the head. Thus ended the life of this man of integrity who did not hesitate to die for his ideals.

However, the long list of crimes was not at an end. Another member of Congress, the senator from Chiapas, Doctor Belisario Domínguez, made an extraordinary speech in which he denounced the crimes and abuses perpetrated by General Huerta. On September 23, he presented his speech to the members of the Directorate who returned it to him, saying that since knowledge of the accusations against the Executive Branch was no concern of the Senate, he should take it to the corresponding authority, which in this case was the Chamber of Deputies. In reality, they were afraid to have the speech delivered and therefore tried to avoid its publication. Senator Domínguez decided to publish and distribute his speech, but because he was unable to find a printer, he made copies on a typewriter, asking the reader to retype it on his own. Soon he wrote another speech which at long last was printed by a young woman and circulated secretly. We quote fragments of both speeches as they show Senator Domínguez's civil courage in daring to expose the chaotic and shameful situation which the country was going through. In the first speech he said:

"The truth is this: During the Government of Don Victoriano Huerta not only has nothing been done to attain peace in the country, but the present condition of the Republic is infinitely worse than before. Revolution has spread to almost all the States. Many nations, who were good friends of Mexico before, refuse to recognize its government because it is an illegal one. Our currency has devaluated abroad, our credit is extremely bad; the entire Mexican press has been muzzled or has cowardly sold itself to the Government by systematically not revealing the truth; our fields are abandoned; many towns have been razed; and, lastly, hunger and misery are rampant and threaten to spread rapidly over the entire surface of our unfortunate Nation. Who has caused this sad situation?"

"In the first place, and above all, the Mexican people cannot afford to have Don Victoriano Huerta as the President of the Republic, the soldier who seized power by means of treachery and whose first deed upon taking over the office of president was to murder in a cowardly manner the legal President and Vice-President who were appointed by popular vote. The dead President bestowed on Victoriano Huerta sundry promotions, honors and distinctions, believing in his public avowal of unswerving loyalty and allegiance to him."

"Secondly, this grievous situation is a result of the methods employed by Don Victoriano Huerta for the achievement of peace. You all know what these methods are: extermination and death for all men whether they be families or individuals— who do not sympathize with his government."

In the second speech, he states:

"And, Honorable Senators, this policy of terror (he referred to the policy applied against the Zapata troops in the State of Morelos) is employed by Don Victoriano Huerta because, in the first place, he is a narrow-minded old soldier and therefore cannot believe there might be other ways of doing things; secondly, because of the path he has taken to come to power and the events which have occurred during his government, Don Victoriano Huerta's mind is unbalanced, his spirit is misguided, lost and confused."

These two speeches provoked Huerta's ire and he decided to eliminate Domínguez. The senator had a premonition that his end was near, since in a letter to Mr. Jesús Fernández, he said:

"I know that my life is in danger and, since murder by the government is the order of the day, I am prepared for anything."

"I would appreciate it if you would deliver the enclosed page to Richard (his son). It contains my last instructions. You will deliver it to him at noon day after tomorrow, which is Wednesday. If by that time nothing new has happened, I shall contact you so that you can return the page to me. You must deliver it to Richard without anyone seeing you. I beg you not to try to get in touch with me or Richard until Wednesday. Many tranks. Goodbye. Yours truly, Belisario Domínguez (signature)..."

His hunch was right; he was soon murdered by orders of Doctor Urrutia, Secretary of the Interior and an intimate friend of Huerta.

Let us now go back to the battlefields where the military chapters that would put an end to Huerta's spurious government would be written.

Let us take a look at the actions and legal measures which the Commander-in-Chief, Carranza, would adopt. On May 24th in Piedras Negras, Coahuila, he put in effect the Law of January 25, 1862, which had been dictated by President Juárez to "punish offenses perpetrated against the Nation, against law and order, and against personal rights. This sole article stated:

"As of the publication of this decree, the law of January 25, 1862 will be put in effect in order to judge General Victoriano Huerta and his accomplices, the promoters and parties responsible for the military attacks which occurred in the capital of the Republic during February of this year, and any parties which in an official or private way have recognized or aided, or will recognize or aid, the so-called government of General Victoriano Huerta, and any other party mentioned in said law."

On June 24, also in Piedras Negras, he decreed the establishment of the first departments of the Treasury and War, dependent on the Offices of the Commander-in-Chief.

On July 4 in Monclova, Coahuila, he decreed the initial organization of the Constitutionalist Army. This decree is very important because it was the foundation of the new army. It stated:

"Venustiano Carranza, Commander-in-Chief of the Constitutionalist Army informs all the inhabitants:

"That in complete command of the ample powers which I have been invested with, I have deemed it necessary to decree and declare the following: Article First. For the organization and operations of the Constitutionalist Army, seven Army Corps are created which shall be named: Northwestern Army Corps; Northeastern Army Corps; Eastern Army Corps; Western Army Corps; Central Area Army Corps; Southern Army Corps, and Southeastern Army Corps."

In Article Second the geographical limits of the new Great Units were established and in Article Third it was ordered that each Corps would be under the orders of a Commanding General.

Our story is concerned solely with the operations and campaigns of the Northwestern Army Corps, commanded by General Alvaro Obregón; those of the famous Northern Division, commanded by General Francisco Villa; and those of the Northeastern Army Corps, commanded by General Pablo González.

We shall outline the actions taken by General Alvaro Obregón who was undoubtedly the most capable general produced by the Revolution. But, who was Obregón? What was he like? John W. Dulles in his book "Yesterday in Mexico", describes him thus: "A very sagacious man, Obregón, Commander of the Constitutionalist Forces in the west, went from victory to victory, demonstrating the qualities which would make him the greatest military commander in the history of Mexico. Besides being an energetic leader and planning his military operations intelligently, he had qualities of plain camaraderie which inspired great devotion to him on the part of his officers and soldiers. One of his first victories over the Huerta federals took place in Santa Rosa, Sonora, in May 1913. The roll call of the subordinates of Obregón taking part in a battle would include names of men destined to go very far..." Let us read another description of this man: "Then the taking up of arms became a necessity and Obregón, who had never practiced the laborious art of war, became a soldier —and what a soldier! He had an admirable knack for organizing men, showing them discipline and serenity in the face of danger, above all, exemplifying his teachings in a myriad different ways, showing them how the attributes of man and citizen should be integrated in the soldier."

In essence, this is the man who will engage in significantly important battles in western Mexico.

The principal army engagements were the Battle of Santa Rosa (May 9 to 11, 1913, waged against federal forces commanded by General Luis Medina Barrón. The revolutionary forces triumphed after a tenacious struggle on both sides. This victory gave Obregón control of the rich Yaqui Valley. Because of this success, Colonel Obregón was promoted to brigadier general on May 21.

Then came the Ortiz Maneuver and the Battle of Santa María (June 19 to 26, 1913). It is interesting to note that on this occasion an aerial reconnaissance was made for the first time ever on an enemy position. Actually, a French aviator named Didier Mason, flying for the constitutionalist troops, discovered that the federals had left their communications line uncovered, which permitted General Obregón to plan a maneuver against the rear guard.

The revolutionary forces confronted the federalists, who were commanded by General Pedro Ojeda, whom Obregón knew personally and had defeated at the border town of Naco a few months before. Huerta had given Ojeda the command of the Yaqui Division. The defeat which Obregón had inflicted on Ojeda was disastrous, since the constitutionalists captured all enemy artillery, 728 prisoners, 200 grenades, 530 rifles, five machine guns, 190,000 cartridges, 25 transport cars and many other war supplies. The defeat had been enormous; General Juan Barragán in his book *Military History of the Revolution and of the Constitutionalist Army,* says: "The struggle had acquired a tragic character for the federalists, especially when, deprived of their water supply, they became unbearably thirsty and disobeying their leaders, threw themselves on some watermelon fields that were a perfect blank for the revolutionary riflemen who were able to pick them out while they were completely defenseless. Dead federal soldiers were found by the hundreds, their mouths still glued to the fresh watermelons."

On the 26th General Ojeda managed to arrive at the port of Guaymas with his shattered troops; the city was besieged for the rest of the struggle. Not until July 1914 did the federal troops evacuate it.

Meantime, General Obregón decided to continue his advance to the south in order to join other rebel groups operating in the States of Sinaloa and Nayarit. it.

Once in Sinaloa, his troops together with other revolutionary groups, captured Culiacán, forcing the federalists to retreat to the port of Mazatlán. Just as had happened in Guaymas, there they would remain shut in for the duration of the war.

General Obregón continued his victorious campaign to the south, going into the territory of Tepic, where several revolutionary leaders operated, among which was the famous general, Rafael Buelna, the "Little Grain of Gold". On May 16, 1914, Tepic fell —thus all the territory was now in the hands of the constitutionalists. From this

*A Federal train bombarded
by revolutionaries.*

point on, the campaign in Jalisco began. It is in this state where several of the decisive battles in Mexican revolutionary history would be fought. In effect, here Obregón confronted the Western Division, commanded by a general well advanced in years, José M. Mier. Perhaps these battles came the closest to resembling what is thought of as the classic battle in which the maneuver plays a brilliant role. We refer to the battles of Orendáin-La Venta, where the federal general, Miguel Bernad was defeated, and El Castillo (July 6-8) where General Mier, who died in action, was defeated. With these very important victories, all of western Mexico was in the hands of the constitutionalists, since quite soon the federal redoubt in Colima would be eliminated, and consequently, Obregón leading his Army Corps would sweep into the capital of the Republic.

Now let us go on to briefly detail the actions of the legendary Northern Division, commanded by Francisco Villa.

We should remember that Villa had returned to Mexico on March 9 with only a small band of men to initiate an incredible military career. He would become one of the most-discussed men of the Revolution.

Commander-in-Chief Carranza had already heard of Villa with regard to his participation in the Madero Revolution and subsequently in the campaign against Pascual Orozco. Therefore, he realized how important it was for Villa to join the cause. So, he sent an emissary to Ciudad Camargo to interview Villa and offer him the rank of brigadier general. Villa accepted the rank conferred on him and also the fact that Carranza was Commander-in-Chief, but he did not accept being a subordinate to Obregón's Army Corps, nor did he accept Manuel Chao as

Governor of the State. Once he was recognized as a constitutionalist general, Villa proceeded to organize the Brigade which would bear his name and be the mainstay of the Northern Division.

His penchant for war was soon evidenced as he fought in the central and northern areas of the State of Chihuahua.

Broadly-speaking, let us see who this man Villa was. This singular person was a typical product of the people: of very humble origins, Villa was endowed with a great personality, with charisma; he was an unquestionable leader of men; his lack of culture was substituted by a marvellous native intelligence; a naturally charming man, he was undoubtedly the most popular figure of the Mexican Revolution.

Discussed profoundly, he was praised by some and reviled by others. On more occasions than we care to mention he was unnecessarily cruel, but he was a symbol of those trying days - the story of his campaigns is one full of drama and emotion.

General M.A. Sánchez Lamego in his book *Military History of the Mexican Revolution*, describes him like this: "General Villa, who possessed little or no culture, was impulsive, haughty, tenacious and bloody. He exercised command by means of violence and terror. He would threaten his subordinates with death if they were unable to comply with the missions entrusted them.

The brothers Luis and Adrián Aguirre Benavides in their book *The Great Battles of the Northern División*, described him as follows: "From a military point of view, Villa was then the most powerful man of his times and surely the most capable and audacious which our century has produced..." This contradictory man was appointed

Commander of the Northern Division in a meeting held in Ciudad Jiménez during the second half of September 1913.

At the head of his forces, Villa marched to Torreón, "Pearl of the Lagoon", an important communications and commercial center which was garrisoned by the Nazas Division commanded by General Eutiquio Munguía with approximately 3,500 men. The preliminary operations were the battles of Avilés and Lerdo, which took place on September 29th. The federalists were defeated in these battles and federal General Felipe Alvírez lost his life.

From September 30 and October 1, furious battles raged between the federals and revolutionaries, the former being defeated. General Munguía painfully evacuated the city with 1,700 men, which was what was left of the federal force which had fought at Torreón. As soon as he arrived at the capital, the defeated general was court-martialed by the express orders of Huerta: it was thought that the defense had not been adequate.

After his victory in Torreón, Villa returned to Chihuahua, leaving the fallen city in the command of Colonel Calixto Contreras. The State Capital was garrisoned by the Northern Federal Division commanded by Brigadier General Salvador Mercado. In those days the Huerta Government only controlled the cities of Chihuahua and Juárez; the former had a small garrison, and the latter had federal forces of 6,300 men divided among the three arms, with nine units of artillery and four machine guns.

The struggle to seize the capital began on November 5, but the revolutionaries were pushed back after two days of fighting. Villa apparently had ordered retreat and then he had an idea. He would launch an audacious surprise attack: the capture of Ciudad Juárez, located 360 kilometers from the capital. During the attack, the Villa forces were able to enter the sleeping city at dawn (on the 15th), the train unloaded Villa troops and within minutes they were able to diminish the surprised Huerta garrison considerably. The soldiers who were neither taken prisioner nor killed escaped to El Paso, becoming prisoners of United States forces. The capture of Ciudad Juárez was of great importance from a military viewpoint as well as a psychological one; the Villa revolutionaries, in an incredibly audacious attack, had come into possession of one of the most important border towns, which would open up a door to introduce arms, ammunition and supplies of all kinds. When General Mercado was informed that the Villa troops had passed by in the direction of the north, he sent reinforcements to Ciudad Juárez which did not arrive in time. However, these reinforcements were forced to engage in battle at Tierra Blanca (a railroad station 32 kilometers to the south of Ciudad Juárez). Here, one of the bloodiest battles fought by the Northern Division occurred. It was a total victory for Villa, who defeated the federalists commanded by Generals Mancilla, José Inés Salazar, Marcelo Caraveo and others. This defeat sealed the fate of the capital, since General Mercado was closed in completely with no hopes of getting reinforcements, making it necessary for him to order the evacuation of the city. The troops withdrew to the north and were defeated in Ojinaga in the course of two combats, the first taking place on December 31 and the second on Jaunary 4, 1914. The federal defeat was complete and brought as a consequence the annihilation of the government division and the absolute control by Pancho Villa of the enormous State of Chihuahua.

After a rest, the troops commanded by Villa again took the offensive against the city of Torreón, which at the end of the previous year (1913) had been recaptured by the federalists commanded by General José Refugio Velasco.

In the last few days of March, the revolutionary troops started advancing on Torreón. After a few reconnaissance fights, action was seen in Tlahualilo and Sacramento, as follows:

The battles of San Pedro de las Colonias and of Porvenir (March 22); the battle of Gómez Palacio (March 22-27) and the attack and seizure of Torreón (March 27 to April 2).

This was one of the most sanguinary battles in the history of the Mexican Revolution, and resulted in the taking of this important city. Later the Northern Division continued its advance and engaged in another bloody battle in San Pedro de las Colonias from April 10 to 13, against the federal forces. Villa stayed there to rest for approximately two months, until he got orders from Carranza to capture Saltillo. This resulted in a new battle at Paredón, a place near Saltillo, where the Federalists, commanded by General Ignacio Muñoz, were defeated. When General Joaquín Maass was informed of the bad news, he ordered the evacuation of Saltillo to the city of San Luis Potosí. During these battles a few prominent generals like Felipe Angeles and Maclovio Herrera, among others, played important roles. Angeles a much-discussed figure of the Revolution, is described as follows: "His ineptitude for court life, his repudiation of everything which smacked of servility, made him fail just as he had joined the revolutionary movement initiated against the Usurper Huerta. Francisco Villa welcomes him with great respect. Compared with Villa, a man in an uncultivated state, Angeles symbolized understanding, a cultivated intelligence, the concept of civic life, a high moral standard which attempts to organize into a real and organic structure the vague, diffuse and romantic yearnings for national improvement. To Maclovio Herrera, one of the strong arms of the Villa movement at that time, Angeles was: "Not a learned man, but intelligent. In the daily peril of battles, he quickly learns that the duties of a soldier hold high moral and constitutional values. He will not wage war for war's sake. He will fight to destroy the semi-feudal system which still exists and he will be a convinced land reformer. He will go to the front with the conviction that the country must be reconstructed with new laws and new elements."

Let us go on to outline the final operations of the powerful Northern Division against the Federal Army.

Zacatecas was considered a very important city because it obstructed the advance toward the central area of the country. It had to be captured. General Pánfilo Natera had made useless attempts to do just this. For this reason, Carranza ordered Pancho Villa to reinforce the troops of Generals Arrieta and Natera with the 5,000 men commanded by General José I. Robles. Villa opposed this plan and decided to march with his Division to the conquest of this important mining city. This action would ultimately result in the rupture of the constitutionalist forces. However, Villa together with his most important generals marched on Zacatecas which was garrisoned by 7,000 federalists commanded by General Luis Medina Barrón. In a spectacular and extremely bloody battle, the Villa troops became the victors on June 23, 1914. The battle was a veritable hecatomb for Huerta's followers: the artillery caused much destruction in the city and in the federal ranks; a great number of federal soldiers were killed. With great hardship the commander and a group of generals and soldiers escaped to Aguascalientes.

After this significant victory, the Northern Division about-faced, withdrawing to Torreón. So ends the story of this famous unit in its struggle against the Huerta regime.

We shall now outline briefly the operations of the Northeastern Army Corps under the command of General Pablo González. This general operated with changing luck in the States of Nuevo León, Tamaulipas and Coahuila, engaging in combat in Salinas, Victoria, Topo Chico, an assault on Monterrey, an attack and capture of Ciudad Victoria, etc. As a result of this campaign, almost all of the northeastern area of the Republic fell into the hands of General González. Only Monterrey, in Nuevo León, Nuevo Laredo and Tampico, both in Tamaulipas, were still under the Huerta Government. A few of the generals who took part in these battles under the command of González, would later take an active part in the life of the Republic: they were Antonio I. Villarreal, Francisco Murguía, Cesáreo Castro, Eulalio Gutiérrez, Jesús Agustín Castro, and others.

The final operations of the Northern Army Corps were the assault and taking of Monterrey (April 1914) and the assault and taking of Tampico (April 1914). At last, the entire west was in the hands of the constitutionalists.

As a consequence of the actions described above, events run helter-skelter at a rapid pace. After the battles of Orendáin-La Venta and El Castillo, General Victoriano Huerta resigned his post to the Presidency on July 15, leaving in his place Attorney Francisco Carbajal to make the final negotiations and turn over the government to the victorious Revolution. The task of negotiating the Treaties of Teoloyucan, which marked the end of the Federal Army, fell to the hands of Attorney and General Eduardo Iturbide in his capacity as Governor of the Federal District and in

*Young Federal soldiers recruited by the "leva" system.*

representation of Provisional President Carbajal. He was joined in this endeavor by the last commander of the Federal Army, General José Refugio Velasco.

On August 13 while on the way to Teoloyucan from Cuautitlán, these treaties, which would put an end to the Federal Army, were signed on the fender of an automobile. The important document was signed by General Alvaro Obregón and General Lucio Blanco for the Constitutionalist Troops; by General Gustavo A. Salas for the Federal Army; and by Commodore Othón P. Blanco for the National Armada. The illegal government of General Huerta had finally come to an end, and all Mexicans awaited the beginning of a new era of peace with great expectations and hope. How wrong they were! A good deal of the peoples' blood would still be shed before Mexico could find the way to peace and tranquility, for now the struggle between the triumphant factions would begin.

We now must mention an event which would have international consequences. We refer to the occupation of the port of Veracruz by United States troops in April 1914.

That same month an incident occurred in the port of Tampico when a group of U. S. marines was arrested by the federal commander for disturbing the peace. The marines were freed but the United States admiral affirmed that an outrage had been committed against his country and demanded amends, requesting the Mexican Government to give a 21-gun salute to the United States flag. Huerta refused and, after fruitless negotiations, on April 21 the U. S. Marines landed and occupied the port of Veracruz and were resisted bravely by the garrison of cadets of the Heroic Naval Academy and a large group of civilians, once more adding a page of glory to the annals of our history. Huerta tried to capitalize on this unfortunate event, and some of his generals addressed themselves to the revolutionary generals, as did General Joaquín Téllez, commander of the federal garrison at Guaymas, who sent General Obregón the following message: "United States troops made an unlawful landing at Veracruz yesterday, initiating combat. The time has come to forget internal affairs and defend our Nation; I call upon you to unite in an effort to save our country. I expect your frank and faithful reply letting me know how you stand. Joaqun Téllez (signature)." This was Obregón's reply: "Mr. Joaquín Téllez. Guaymas. The abominable crime to the detriment of the Nation which the Traitor and Murderer Huerta has just committed by deliberately provoking a foreign invasion, is unheard of. Civilization, history and the Constitutionalist Army, which is the sole representative of national dignity, will vigorously protest such deeds and if the United States persists in the invasion disregarding the notes that our dignified chief Don Venustiano Carranza has sent to President Wilson, the Constitutionalist Army, to which I have the honor of belonging, shall fight to the last man against it, thereby saving national dignity; this you cannot do because you have trampled it. Therefore, as you can see, we are unwilling to join a corrupt army that can only negotiate pacts with treason and crime. If you are invaded at said port by United States ships and defeated, as you usually are, you will be permitted to retreat to a predetermined place where you will remain until you receive instructions from the Chief Executive regarding your fate. Commanding General. Alvaro Obregón."

What Huerta was actually trying to do was to make the Constitutionalists abandon their rebel attitude and join his government. When the futility of this dawned on him, he tried to incite the naturally patriotic feelings of the Mexican people in an effort to increase enlistment, the difference being that the volunteers would be sent to fight the Constitutionalists and not the invaders.

Instances of courage abounded at the port of Veracruz. Cadet Virgilio Uribe and Lieutenant José Azueta, both of the Heroic Naval Academy, were killed, thereby adding another page of glory to that written several years hence by the cadets of the Heroic Military School. Huerta ordered the federal troops commanded by General Gustavo Maass to evacuate the port. However, a few soldiers remained at the port, as did the 19th Infantry Battalion, commanded by Lieutenant Colonel Albino Cerrillo. José Peña F. in his book *Veracruz, Four Times Heroic,* narrates this incident: "Thirsty, weakened by hunger, harrassed by the enemy, aided by their women who gave a high example of abnegation by carrying rifles themselves or stopping the flow of blood from the men's wounds with their rebozos, these soldiers fought ferociously like good Mexicans, unknown and ignored men of the 19th Battalion under the leadership of the courageous Lieutenant Colonel Cerrillo."

A diplomatic solution was looked for. A group of Mexican and American diplomats met in the city of Niagara Falls. Representatives of Brazil, Argentina and Chile were also invited to participate. However, no final agreement of compromise was signed.

American troops still occupied the port of Veracruz and not until November 22, 1914, upon receiving orders from their government to evacuate the city and return to their ships, did they leave. General Cándido Aguilar, at the head of the Constitutionalist troops, was ordered to reoccupy Veracruz as soon as it was abandoned by the American troops. Thus ended an incident which only deepened old grudges between the two countries.

# 6

Ruptures in the Revolution. The Conventions of Mexico City and Aguascalientes. Conventionists (Villa Movement). Against Constitutionalists (Carranza Movement). The Conventionist Presidents and Commander-in-Chief Venustiano Carranza. The law of January 6, 1915. General Obregón occupies Mexico City. Prologue to the decisive battles against the Villa Movement.

After the occupation of Mexico City by the revolutionaries and because Carranza was firmly installed in power as Chief Executive, the differences between Villa and Carranza, which had been dormant, became evident. The reader will remember that even before the Battle of Zacatecas in June, 1914, there were differences between both men. To this we should add that Villa was at the height of his fame and was adulated by a group of politicians; this had made him exceedingly arrogant. Carranza, who was more balanced and serene, tried to avoid the inevitable: the division of the Revolutionary movement into two large factions which would only serve to bring more death and pain to the poor Mexican people.

Even before the final defeat of the Huerta movement, Carranza, conscious that he needed Villa's cooperation and wishing to avoid the rupture which in the long run would have helped their common enemy, decided to negotiate. Therefore, he dispatched a delegation to the city of Torreón, which was the General Headquarters of Villa. The delegation was made up of Generals Antonio I. Villarreal, Cesáreo Castro and Luis Caballero. On his own behalf, Villa designated General José I. Robles, Dr. Manuel Silva and Engineer Manuel Bonilla. After much discussion, an agreement was reached and a document called the Torreón Pact was signed, ratifying the Northern Division's allegiance to Mr. Carranza. Apparently, this resolved the problem of the Unit's collective insubordination regarding the events which culminated in the Battle of Zacatecas.

The Eighth Clause was the most important portion of this document. Andrés Molina Enríquez called it the "Golden Clause", stating that it was "The highest point reached by both mestizos and Indians since the Declaration of Independence by Morelos to the present time with regard to the earnest desire to make agrarian reforms a reality in order to give economic support to their nationalization.

EIGHTH: "As the present rebellion is a struggle of the disinherited against the abuses of the powerful and realizing that the causes of the misfortunes afflicting the country are derived from pretorianism (abuse of political power exercised by a group of the military), plutocracy and the clergy, the Northern and Northeastern Divisions solemnly resolve to fight until the ex-Federal Army is dissolved completely and is substituted by the Constitutionalist Army; to establish a democratic regime in our Nation; to attain the well-being of workers, to emancipate the farmers from an economic point of view, distributing lands fairly or utilizing other means in order to resolve the agrarian problem; to correct, punish and demand the related responsibilities of the Roman Catholic clergy, who materially or intellectually have aided the Usurper Victoriano Huerta."

Meanwhile, Carranza also endeavored to reach an agreement with Zapata's followers. Therefore, he sent a commission composed of General Antonio I. Villarreal and Attorney Luis Cabrera who met with the Zapata delegates, Attorney Antonio Díaz Soto y Gama, Generals Manuel Palafox and Emiliano Zapata. No agreement was reached in this meeting.

Carranza, upon occupying Mexico City and in agreement with the provisos of the Plan of Guadalupe, settled in the National Palace and took charge of the Executive Power until elections could be held.

Evidently, he appointed a cabinet in which some of his principal collaborators took part. They were: Attorney Isidro Fabela in Foreign Affairs; Attorney Eliseo Arredondo in the Interior Engineer Felícitas Villarreal in the Treasury; Engineer Ignacio Bonillas in Communications; Engineer Félix F. Palavicini in Public Instruction and Fine Arts; Engineer Pastor Rouaix in Development, Colonization and Industry; General Jacinto B. Treviño in War and the Navy; Attorney Manuel Escudero Verdugo in Justice.

Let us go back to the north where Villa did not want to submit to the authority of the new government, retreating to Chihuahua where he had remained with the main body of his troops. General Obregón went to see him there in the hopes of reaching an agreement. On Friday, August 21st, 1914, Huerta left Mexico City for the capital of Chihuahua, Moreover, Huerta should press for a solution to the conflict which was taking shape in Sonora between Governor Maytorena (supported by Villa) and General Salvador Alvarado, Colonel Plutarco Elías Calles and Benjamín Hill. In Chihuahua City, Obregón was met by Raúl Madero, Chao and José Rodríguez; they all went with him to meet with the Commander of the Northern Division. Immediately, the Maytorena case came up for discussion. In order to resolve it, therefore, both generals travelled to Nogales, Sonora, where a temporary solution was reached between Maytorena and Colonel Plutarco Elías Calles. Early in September, Obregón returned to the capital of the Republic accompanied by two of Villa's representatives, Dr. Silva and Attorney Miguel Díaz Lombardo. There, several of Villa's propositions were discussed, but Carranza did not accept them. A few days later Villa insisted on some measures which had not been taken in Sonora and which he wished would be complied with. As a consequence, a second trip was made by Obregón to Chihuahua in order to meet with Villa. On September 16 he again arrived at this northern city and during the renewed talks, a serious incident occurred which almost cost Obregón his life. Villa, in a fit of anger, ordered the Sonora general shot. He finally calmed down and the firing did not take place; if it had, the history of Mexico would have been radically different. What would Villa have given to be able to know his inscrutable destiny? The following year Obregón would defeat him decisively on the plains of Celaya, destroying the mighty Northern Division and the

*A typical revolutionary of that time.*

prestige of its proud leader. However, the future cannot be predicted and Villa pardoned the life of his guest. On September 21st Obregón set out for Mexico City in the company of Generals Eugenio Aguirre, Benavides and José Isabel Robles. Only a few hours had elapsed when their passenger train was brusquely ordered to turn back. What had happened? Carranza had heard about the threat to his emissary's life and had sent a message to Villa, which was written in a violent and peremptory manner. This angered Villa. The train turned back but Villa did not have Obregón shot on this occasion either, and Obregón was able to return to Mexico City on September 26. Villa had spared Obregón's life, but his own fate was sealed.

On the 22nd Villa sent Carranza a telegram which corroborates his insubordination and, as a result, the division of the revolutionary army into two irreconcilable factions. The telegram read:

"General Headquarters in Chihuahua, September 22, 1914. Mr. Venustiano Carranza, México, D. F. In answer to your message, I declare that General Obregón and other generals of this Division last night left for the capital with the purpose of discussing important matters related to the general conditions prevailing in the Republic. However, in view of the procedures employed by you, which reveal a premeditated desire to prevent the satisfactory settlement of all difficulties obstructing peace, which we desire above all, I have given orders to interrupt the trip and to detain them in Torreón. Therefore, I inform you that this Division shall not attend the Convention which you have summoned. I of course declare that we do not recognize you as Commander-in-Chief of the Republic, leaving you at liberty to do as you see fit. Commanding General Francisco Villa."

The break was now definite. No stone was left unturned to reach a peaceful understanding between the two great revolutionary factions; the principal military and political leaders made efforts to negotiate peace. First, a convention to be held in Mexico City was summoned with the object of finding a solution to the conflict; later it was thought that the capital would be an inadequate location for this assembly. Finally, the convention was transferred to the city of Aguascalientes, which was considered neutral territory. However, four heated sessions were actually held in Mexico City, the last one being the most surprising and emotional. In this particular session Carranza presented his resignation of the position charged with Executive Power. He took the floor and addressed the people gathered in the Chamber of Deputies and with a voice full of emotion, he said:

"You conferred upon me the command of the Army, you placed the Executive Power of the Nation in my hands. I cannot deliver these two sacred trusts, as has been requested by a group of leaders, misguided in the performance of their duties, and a few civilians, to whom the Nation owes nothing in this struggle, without dishonor.. I can only deliver it to the leaders herein assembled, and do so at this very moment. I expect your immediate resolution of this matter and shall leave the Convention immediately so that you can feel free to make a decision. I hope this decision will be for the supreme good of the Nation."

Carranza left the chamber in the midst of applause. Attorney Luis Cabrera, one of the idealogists of the Carranza movement and a brilliant orator, then took the floor and again voted for Carranza. There was renewed discussion and, finally, a commission was sent to Carranza's house requesting him to return to the Chamber of Deputies. There he was informed that by a unanimous motion of the Assembly his resignation had not been accepted. Therefore, he continued in charge of the Executive Power. Mr. Carranza replied: "For the time my services are needed I shall endeavor to keep peace in the Nation." After much discussion, on October 5 it was finally decided to transfer the convention to the city of Aguascalientes where the debates of the conventionists would continue.

Work was taken up again on October 10 at the Morelos Theater in Aguascalientes. One hundred delegates took part, among them were 37 delegates of the Northern Division.

The Convention was declared sovereign from the beginning of the sessions. The delegates' signatures were affixed to a national flag. During the first few sessions Zapata's followers were invited as it was decided that without them a unanimous decision could not be reached. On the 27th of the month, the Zapata delegates finally came and work proceeded with them. Two sessions later with the definite support of the Villa faction, the Plan of Ayala was approved by the Convention. It was also decided to give the right to vote to the Zapata delegates. Meantime, Carranza had refused an invitation to attend personally the meetings in Aguascalientes. This caused great commotion. However, the Convention was greatly influenced by the Villa faction, led by General Felipe Angeles, who was also supported by the Zapata delegates. On October 30th a transcendental agreement was reached. The following was declared:

"To the best interests of the Revolution, Citizen Venustiano Carranza will resign from his duties as Commander-in-Chief of the Constitutionalist Army and in charge of the Executive Power, so will Citizen Francisco

Villa as Commanding Chief of the Northern Division. This Convention will proceed to name a provisional president for the Republic who, during the pre-constitutional period, will carry out the social and political reforms which the country needs. The rank of major general shall be bestowed on Citizen Venustiano Carranza as of the date of the Plan of Guadalupe." Naturally, this decision did not meet with the approval of either Carranza or Villa, especially the former when he learned that the Convention had chosen General Eulalio Gutiérrez as Provisional President. Although Villa apparently had decided to comply with the order, he did not do so and proceeded to concentrate his troops on the outskirts of Aguascalientes.

Because he mistrusted General Lucio Blanco's stance, Carranza prudently decided to abandon Mexico City and retire to the port of Veracruz. A few days later, General Obregón, General Villarreal and General Hay caught up with him in Córdoba where they told him of the decision to remove him. Carranza did not accept, in spite of the fact that Eulalio Gutiérrez tried to convince him of his impartiality. As a consequence of his position, things came to a head. Gutiérrez, not having troops, would fall into the hands of Pancho Villa. In effect, the Provisional President made a decision which would put him on the side of Carranza's enemies: he named Villa Commander-in-Chief of the Conventionalist Armies. Carranza and Gutiérrez each launched a manifesto in which one diasvows the other. The Revolution had split and only the use of arms would decide who would be the vanquisher. Carranza went to Veracruz and Eulalio Gutiérrez advanced on the long-suffering capital of the Republic. December 3, 1914, arrived. Three days later the Conventionist Army entered, 50,000-men strong, led by General Villa and General Zapata.

Meantime, a very important event had taken place at Veracruz. Convinced of the futility of their diplomatic efforts, the Americans had decided to evacuate the port. They did so on November 23, 1914. Three days later, on the 26th, Carranza arrived with members of his cabinet and entrenched himself in the Lighthouse Building. There he awaited the course of events.

Carranza, who was a very good judge of men, was sure that the frail alliance between Eulalio Gutiérrez and Villa would not last. He was right. The Provisional President could not even set up the faintest resemblance to a government, hence, Mexico City fell into anarchy, a prey to the radicalism of Villa's troops. General Gutiérrez, convinced that his efforts were to no avail, abandoned the capital with a few troops, which dissolved after a small number of skirmishes. Desperate, General Gutiérrez gave himself up to Carranza's men and was granted amnesty. Howewer, the country was bogged down in anarchy. General Juan Barragán in his bok *History of the Army and the Constitutionalist Revolution,* gives a vivid picture of these months, explaining that Agua Prieta was the sole city under the control of the constitutionalists in the whole state of Sonora; Chihuahua, Coahuila and Nuevo León were under the influence of Villa's army; Tamaulipas was in the hands of troops loyal to Carranza; Nuevo León, Matamoros, Tampico, Veracruz, Campeche, Tabasco and Yucatán were for the Constitutionalists, so was Chiapas; Oaxaca was partly in the hands of the Carranza Government; Guerrero in enemy hands, except for Acapulco; Sinaloa under the control of Villa's followers, except for Mazatlán; and finally, the central States, including the capital of the Nation, in the power of the enemy.

However, while this ominous gloom spread over the landscape and was witnessed by the people, Mr. Carranza strove to organize the country's public affairs. Hence, on January 6, 1915, he published a law which initiated the Land Reform in Mexico. This law, as was asserted so ably by the prominent historian Don Jesús Silva Herzog, is considered the most important agrarian legislation, second only to the laws of disentailment of Church property, which were passed in 1856 and 1859. Attorney Don Luis Cabrera, who undoubtedly had one of the most brilliant minds of that memorable era, played a very important role regarding this law. This prominent attorney from Puebla was the author of the important decree, which, among other things, states:

"Consequently, great masses of the rural population have had no other recourse for obtaining the necessities of life, but to hire themselves out at miserable wages to the powerful landowners; the inevitable outcome has been the conditions of misery, abjection and veritable slavery under which this great number of laborers has lived and still does."

Besides its undeniable merit of bringing much-desired justice to the farmer, this law had a psychological effect in attracting to it "great masses of the rural population" and at the same time detracting these same masses from the Villa movement.

At this time, the convention was going through its last throes of agony: it was dying because of a lack of support. General Gutiérrez was briefly succeeded by General Roque González Garza, who came from the Villa ranks.

General Obregón, with the stamina always characterizing him, organized a new military contingent and, by January 5, 1915, occupied the city of Puebla. On the 28th he again entered the much-chastised capital, which by now had been evacuated by Zapata's troops. There he stayed a few months with the purpose of recruiting, organizing and arming new troops and then marching with them in search of the enemy. He did exactly this, incorporating into his forces the red battalions of workers belonging to the House of World Workers, who would fight with great courage on the plains of Celaya. There were six battalions in all, and they were outstanding. In 1917 when they were discharged by Carranza, he said to them: "Go back to your jobs in an orderly fashion and in peace as the country is deeply grateful to you."

Those months were terrible ones for Mexico City: there was hunger, which of course was felt more sharply by the poor; there was a lack of food; sickness prevailed; and to this was added plundering by revolutionary groups, causing grave problems to the long-suffering city.

The situation was no better in the rest of the country. The north and west were in flames, since furious battles were raging between Villa's men, commanded by Orestes Pereyra, Fierro, Medina, Rosalío Hernández and Angeles, and the Constitutionalists, commanded by Diéguez, Murguía and other generals. Important battles were waged like Atenquique and Ramos Arizpe, and Guadalajara, Jalisco, was taken. This all attested to the ferocious struggle in which thousands of Mexicans were being killed in a sterile war of factions.

The conventionists, as we have previously mentioned, ended up by dispersing. González Garza turned over his appointment, without power, to Attorney Lagos Cházaro. Finally, the remaining conventionists separated, some going to the north and others finding refuge in Zapata's army. Meanwhile, the troops of Villa and Carranza made ready

*Venustiano Carranza, with Generals Obregón, Pesqueira, Coss, Hay and others, in the National Palace after the triumph of the Revolution.*

for the decisive battles. The suffering of the people of Mexico City had not ceased. Again Obregón had decided to evacuate the City of Palaces, as it was called, saying that the city "was not a strategic position, nor a railroad center, nor was it a place where troops could find the necessary provisions for sustenance and war. On the other hand, to guard Mexico City adequately, a large force must be maintained which is actually needed at other points where it can do more good. For this reason, the question of holding or not holding the city is of little importance." The fate of the city had been decided, and in a telegram dated March 9 Obregón says: "At midnight today I shall evacuate Mexico City and will head for the north. . ." This was done true to form and, as the constitutionalists were departing Zapata's army was entering the city from Ajusco and Milpa Alta.

Obregón had decided to march north so that he could engage in  battle with the Villa troops. Villa's men were concentrated in Querétaro, but they had little confidence in themselves as their leader was not with them. So, they decided to withdraw to the State of Guanajuato.

Obregón continued his advance, occupying Querétaro on March 31st; slowly but surely the two formidable enemies approached the plains of Celaya where the fate of the Revolution would be irrevocably sealed.

# 7

Obregón defeats Villa at Celaya, Trinidad, León and Aguascalientes (1915). Consolidation of Carranza. The Santa Isabel and Columbus incidents. The Punitive Expedition. The combat at Carrizal.

Obregón marched with his troops from Querétaro to Celaya with the intention of engaging in a decisive battle against Villa. However, he thought that Pancho Villa would fight in Irapuato and not Celaya.

Villa was quite confident, in spite of General Felipe Angeles's warnings, advising him from the north not to engage in battle. "The day that General Villa suffers defeat in the main body of his ranks, the Northern Division will cease to exist.", he had prophesied. However, the Guerrilla from the North chose to disregard the advice given him by the former federalist general. In broad terms, Villa's position was better than Obregón's. This was due to the fact that Villa's troops controlled the railroad tracks of the northern and central areas of the country, which permitted them to communicate with the different cities under their authority. The constitutionalists did not have this control. We should remember that the Zapata army was at the rear of Obregón's army and, although it was not a large force, it constituted a menace.

On April 4, Obregón troops arrived at Celaya, a city which at that time had 35,000 inhabitants and was one of the richest and most important cities of the Bajío Region.

In his book *Eight Thousand Kilometers of Campaigns,* the Conqueror of Santa Rosa states the following: "Since my departure from Querétaro the total force with which I advanced to the central area of the Republic was eleven thousand men from the three armed forces: artillery, 13 thick-caliber cannon and 86 machine guns; 6,000 mounted and foot cavalry; 5,000 men, including artillery personnel utilized for service and support." Actually, Carranza's troops were well armed, with abundant ammunition. They had a decisive factor in their favor: excellent commanders. Their generals were better prepared than Villa's. Above all, the undeniable military capacity of General Obregón would be the decisive factor in winning the battle which, in a first analysis, could be considered lost for the constitutionalists.

Villa's Army was at that time superior to the Constitutionalist Army. Numerically, it had 22,000 men; morale was high since it controlled practically all of the Republic; its armaments were good; there was sufficient ammunition; artillery was abundant and efficiently commanded by ex-Federal officers and cavalry officers; its fame was well established because of the very violent charges which had become legendary. These charges were Pancho Villa's most powerful weapon, and his success depended on them.

The fighting started almost immediately. On April 5 the Constitutionalist Generals Alejo González and Alfredo Elizondo captured Acámbaro, while another constitutionalist column commanded by Generals Jesús Novoa and Porfirio González was ordered to destroy the San Luis railroad tracks at Enpalme González.

General Obregón remained in Celaya while the vanguard of his army marched to Guaje (18 kilometers from Celaya), a distance which was far too long for a security detachment.

of General Obregón's military operations, accurately states the following: "...none of the battles engaged in by General Obregón had such a bad beginning as this first one at Celaya. He had already fallen victim to a strategic subterfuge when he thought that the confrontation would occur at Irapuato. This supposition made him disperse his cavalry several travelling-days' distance from his flanks..." Actually, in a telegram dated April 4, 1915, Obregón told Carranza: "Apaseo, Guanajuato, April 4, 1915. Mr. V. Carranza, Veracruz. I believe it is necessary to publish previous message in full in order to confuse the enemy as this is the sole purpose of maneuvers which I mentioned to you. I shall march on Irapuato with whole army. Please publish this information in the United States so it will reach the enemy faster. Greetings. Respectfully. Commanding General. Alvaro Obregón." It is obvious by this communication that Obregón believed the skirmish would take place in Irapuato. On the 5th he was informed that General Villa was in Salamanca where he was reviewing his troops.

On the 6th Villa had already decided to stamp out General Obregón's Army and began his advance from Salamanca in three columns: Cavalry, commanded by General Agustín Estrada, which advanced from the north; Infantry, commanded by Generals José Herón González, Dionisio Triana, Bracamontes and San Román, which advanced from the central area; Cavalry, commanded by General Abel Serratos, which advanced from the south; and Artillery, which marched from the central rear guard.

The first encounter took place on the dawn of the 6th. Villa's troops clashed against the brigade of Maycotte (who was in Celaya) at Guaje. Their commander hurriedly joined his troops, who could scarcely defend themselves as they were attacked by the main body of Villa's troops. When Maycotte observed the critical situation, he informed General Obregón of the crisis. Obregón ordered immediate reinforcements, dispatching General Manuel Laveaga with 1,500 men. However, when he became aware of the seriousness of the situation, he decided to go personally. He reached Guaje at midday only to witness the defeat of his troops. In spite of this, Obregón, showing great will power, with the help of Maycotte was able to withdraw the troops in an orderly fashion. Thus he avoided the frantic flight of his soldiers. Action ended at 4:00 p.m. that same day.

Before we continue, some comments are in order concerning this first skirmish. General Obregón's capabiliites were made evident in this instance when he prevented the defeat from turning into a disorderly disbandment in the face of the relentless advance of Villa's Army. The consequences in morale and material loss resulting from a complete defeat would have been disastrous for his troops stationed in Celaya. That same day General Obregón sent a message to Mr. Carranza informing him of this crucial situation: "Celaya, Guanajuato, April 6, 1915. Mr. V. Carranza, Commander-in-Chief of the Constitutionalist Army, Veracruz. I am honored to communicate to you that the combat at Guaje, commanded by General Maycotte has become more widespread. General Maycotte is in very serious trouble. I am leaving immediately with infantry and machine guns. Our position in battle is not favorable. Therefore counterattack should be quick and consequently irregular; I shall only follow this strategy because more than 3,000 men are involved. Affectionate greetings. Commanding General. Alvaro Obregón."

The Villa troops, using the victory to their advantage, pressed impetuously forward, attacking Celaya. At this point the first of many tactical mistakes made by the attackers occurred since they did not change their strategy of attack, nor did they wait for the much-needed artillery support. Before he departed, General Obregón had ordered General Benjamín Hill, at the head of the infantry, to begin organizing the terrain and have his troops take up strategic positions, which he did. Therefore, when Villa's men confronted the Obregón positions at approximately 5:00 p.m. they encountered a line of fire. There was some hesitation on the right flank of the constitutionalists, which was resolved by a violent cavalry charge which thrust against the Villa cavalry, commanded by General Agustín Estrada. In the late afternoon of that same day the Villa charge lessened, thanks to the efficient coordination of the rifle company, machine gun unit and artillery support.

The last attacks were carried out at 6:00 p.m., ending two hours later. These attacks were fully supported by the main body of the Villa artillery which, firing at night, shot and wasted cartridges.

When night came, the Obregón troops took an inventory to see how they stood. It was more to their disadvantage: the defeat at Guaje; losses totalling 1,500 men, though, fortunately, the majority of these had scattered and during the night they again joined their units; and the city which was practically surrounded by an imposing force. The situation was critical and a few generals advised Obregón to retreat to Querétaro. Commanding General Obregón again sent a telegram to the Commander-in-Chief, saying: "Celaya, April 6, 1915. Mr. V. Carranza. Faros, Veracruz. I am honored to inform you that the battle continues. Cavalries have been defeated. At this time, 11:00 p.m., we have suffered losses of perhaps 2000 men. Enemy attacks quite severe. You can rest assured that while I have a soldier and a bullet left, I will know how to do my duty and will consider it an honor if death should surprise me while fighting crime. Respectfully, Commanding General. A. Obregón."

In spite of these somber presages, the Commanding General stood his ground and refused to retreat, ordering Generals Alfredo Elizondo, Alejo González and Porfirio González to march at full speed to Celaya and reinforce the garrison with their troops. At about the same time Mr. Carranza ordered the immediate dispatch of diverse reinforcements.

In the small hours of the 7th, the brigades of General Elizondo and General González arrived suddenly and the situation seemed to have improved for the constitutionalists.

General Grajales, in his analysis of this battle, points out that: "The combat plan laid out by General Villa for the attack of the following day (April 7) implicitly con-

*General Francisco Villa, General Alvaro Obregón and General John J. Pershing. At the latter's side, Lieutenant Patton, Adjutant to Pershing at that time.*

*First agrarian distribution. In Tamaulipas in 1913, General Lucio Blanco and Major Francisco Mújica allocate parcels of land from Felix Diaz's hacienda "Los Borregos"*

tained the seed of defeat. There isn't the remotest notion of a maneuver in the distribution of his forces; there is no objective of achieving an advantage in a particular section and direction; there is no evidence, not even an expressed wish, to form a general reserve. The action would be simultaneous and uniform along the entire front. . ."

This was actually the case. The attack was conceived as a frontal collision made by three infantry brigades (Bracamontes, Triana and González), supported on a lesser scale by three cavalry brigades (De. la Peña, Reyes and San Román), all supported by the artillery divided into two batteries in combat positions.

The attack commenced that day at dawn. It soon acquired the characteristic violence of Villa's troops, who showed an absolute disregard for life, attacking time and again to collide against a wall of fire composed of Yaquis and other troops. At 9:00 a.m. in the northern constitutionalist sector a crisis occurred due to the lack of ammunition. General Obregón saw the danger and personally ordered opportune reinforcements and expedited rearmament; he then resorted to subterfuge —nowadays we would call it psychological warfare. He ordered a young bugler, Jesús Martínez of the 9th Battalion to sound a rallying blast, which created confusion in Villa's ranks.

As a result of this, another problem surged. Colonel Kloss, commander of the constitutionalist artillery, ordered a quick retreat of his forces, a decision which almost got him shot. Luckily things were clarified and this drastic measure was not put into practice.

Meanwhile, General Villa, realizing the meaning behind these actions, ordered a general attack. The writer Martín Luis Guzmán, in his book *Memoirs of Pancho Villa,* puts these words in Villa's mouth: "These are my orders. As the right and left lines launch their attack, the center line will seize the abandoned positions, and, since the enemy's resistance will be weak at this point, we shall envelop and annihilate them." This plan was put into practice. Villa's men advanced again to the attack, and once more they were thrust back. By this time, it was quite evident that morale was low and the attackers were fatigued.

At midday the constitutionalists took the offensive. The constitutionalist cavalry, commanded by Generals Cesáreo Castro, Maycotte, González and Novoa charged forward en masse carrying out a double envelopment against the enemy. This unexpected movement caused confusion among the worn-out Villa troops, who began to retreat. Soon the retreat turned into a disbandment. Pursuit could not be conducted to advantage as was intended because the cavalry was exhausted and the type of terrain was unfavorable.

The decimated Villa army retired to Salamanca in order to reorganize, get reinforcements and care for the wounded, but, above all, to prepare for a new operation. The first Battle of Celaya had ended with a notable victory for General Obregón, but the fighting had not · yet ended, as Villa would not give up so easily.

Both sides prepared to engage in what is now known as the Second Battle of Celaya. The Obregón forces were appropriately reinforced. They were augmented by the first Eastern Division, sections of the Gavira Brigade, sections of the Gonzalo Novoa Brigade, two workers' battalions, the cavalry brigades of General Porfirio González and General Jesús Novoa, and General Joaquín Amaro's Brigade. With these elements, the troops of the Operational Army were increased to 15,000 men (8,000 cavalry) with 13 pieces of artillery and 86 machine guns. An important convoy of ammunition commanded by General Norzagaray arrived on the 11th — this solved the problem of ammunition.

On his side, Villa did what was needed. He too received reinforcements: the brigades of José I. Prieto and José Ruiz arrived; the troops of César Moya; infantry troops; cavalry and artillery from Jalisco; and elements at the command of Francisco Carrera Torres and Pánfilo Natera, as well as important shipments of ammunition which were sent to him by his brother Hipólito.

The second battle commenced on the 13th. Everything was ready on Obregón's side. The type of terrain was utilized to its maximum because it was furrowed by a great number of ditches and irrigation canals; this would serve as a magnificent obstacle against Villa's cavalry. This cavalry advanced in two groups, one to the north and the other to the south of the railroad; the infantry, which had been transported by train, disembarked at Crespo Station; the artillery marched at the rear of the infantry. The battle started at 5:00 p.m. with scattered skirmishes and reconnaissance actions. Just then General Obregón sent the following message to Mr. Carranza: "...Celaya, April 13, 1915. Commander-in-Chief of Constitutionalist Army. Veracruz. I am honored to inform you that at this very moment fighting has begun. Commanding General. A. Obregón."

The Obregón troops had spread out in a circle as planned. The cavalry stayed outside the combat area, conveniently positioned for attack, as it was destined to deliver the decisive blow.

By 6:00 p.m. the battle had spread, and the tactics followed by the attackers were only a carbon copy of the former battle: ferocious frontal attacks and violent cavalry charges which smashed against the infantry fire. Both artilleries became deadlocked in an artillery fire duel, which would continue far into the night.

The 14th brought much of the same: Villa's men did not slacken their assault, as they were undoubtedly looking for a loophole that would permit a break-through. Thus ended the second day of battle in which both sides were greatly weakened after this devastating skirmish. However, General Obregón knew that at this pace Villa's men would suffer a tremendous loss of blood in a short time and that he would take the offensive at his precise moment.

By dawn of the 15th, the constitutionalist troops took the offensive. The enemy was put off balance and over-whelmingly surprised. Obregón himself marched at the head of the attacking forces.

Immediately the battle became more widespread and the Villa troops, although disconcerted, fought bravely, but on the north they were ousted from Crespo Station and retreated to the Trojes Hacienda. In the central area and the south, the constittutionalist troops forced the Villa soldiers to retreat more swiftly. The nucleus of troops cut off at Trojes clung to a lost position.

Villa's defeat was soon a foregone conclusion. The enemy retreated helter-skelter as the double envelopment conducted by 6,000 cavalry soldiers had put a definite end to the battle. This time the constitutionalists followed in pursuit, thus crowning the brilliant victory. As the after-noon fell, gains and losses were tallied. The constitution-alist casualty figures were 138 dead and 276 wounded; the Villa figures were 4,000 dead, 5,000 wounded, 5,000 prisioners, all the artillery gone (38 cannon), 5,000 firearms of different calibres lost, and 1,000 saddle horses lost. In addition, two generals were executed (Manuel Bracamontes and Joaquín Bauche Alcalde) as well as 130 leaders and officers.

By nightfall of that same day the battle had come to a conclusion; the forces defending Carranza were the victors. It should be mentioned that the two battles near Celaya are considered the largest engagements fought on the American continent, except for the ones fought during the War of Secession (Civil War) in the United States.

On April 16th Villa arrived at Aguascalientes where he concentrated his forces. There he discovered that General Murguía and General Diéguez had joined with General Obregón, taking 10,000 men with them, increasing Obregón's forces to 30,000 men. Villa also reinforced his troops, which increased to a total of 35,000 men. Again he did not listen to the advice of Angeles who suggested that he engage in battle at Aguascalientes. On the contrary, Villa ordered a reconnaissance mission between the cities of León and Silao in order to find an adequate location for the decisive battle. At the end of April, the constitutionalist soldiers took a few towns and ranches near Silao; General Murguía stationed himself with his cavalry in the town of Romita, which was ten kilometers to the west of Trinidad Station. Obregón's rear guard, commanded by General Maycotte, also stationed itself in Naples Station. Obregón was planning to advance on Trinidad, and from there march on to León to, dislodge Villa's men.

On Thursday, April 29, after a combat between the forces of Villa and Murguía, Obregón decided to advance on Trinidad. He attacked but was resisted; he finally reached Naples Station where his vanguard was stationed. By Friday, May 7, Obregón had established his General Headquarters at Trinidad. From this day on there were daily combats. On June lst, Villa's men made a bold attack on Silao, Santa Ana del Conde, and other less important points. This made Murguía and Castro pressure Obregón to attack decisively in order to end the campaign successfully. On June 3rd, while the attack was being prepared, a cannon shot fell in Santa Ana del Conde, tearing General Obregón's arm off and seriously wounding him. General Hill was put in charge; he decided to attack the city of León on the 5th. Villa's men resisted savagely but in vain as the city fell, overpowered by General Murguía. General Juan Barragán in his book *History of the Army and the Constitutionalist Revolution* expresses the following regarding this courageous general: "Just as the victory of Celaya was solely due to the military genius of General Alvaro Obregón who was consecrated with the glorious title of "Hero of Celaya", so we should say with identical moral concern that the brilliant expedition into León which culminated in the complete defeat of Francisco Villa's Army, was due to the valor, ability and decision of General Francisco Murguía."

Obregón continued his advance to the city of Aguascalientes where Villa had concentrated his troops in the hopes of successfully confronting the constitutionalists. On July 10, the Carranza forces defeated the Villa troops, ending at last the bloody campaign which had begun in Celaya. The Villa casualties were 1,500 dead and wounded; 2,000 prisoners; 5,000 men estimated as scattered. Eight trains, four million cartridges, nine cannon, 22 machine guns and 4,000 rifles were captured. The Northern Division in its capacity as a great combat unit had ceased to exist. Obregón himself describes it as follows:

"There is no question that the Northern Division resisted strongly in Aguascalientes, but in reality what it fought for at this town in the middle of the Republic, was the enormous prestige of General Villa, since it was no longer possible to hold back the advance of General Obregón, whose army had grown considerably, benefiting from the desertions of Villa's men, the negative attitude of some of his leaders like Urbina, Natera and Rosalío Hernández, the lack of sufficient war supplies which by now were being denied by the United States."

Although Villa definitely headed for the north, some of his second lieutenants like Fierro and Reyes caused problems in the middle section of the Republic but were finally defeated. Carranza was aware that it was necessary to reoccupy Mexico City, capital of the Republic and the principal economic, social and industrial center as well. Therefore, he commanded General Pablo González to fight the Villa forces, but especially the Zapata forces, who occupied the Valley of Mexico. After a short campaign, the constitutionalist troops again entered the capital on August 2, 1915. The remainder of 1915 would be dedicated to a series of battles between constitutionalist and Villa troops, which were slowly but surely won by the former. Hence, the middle section and the north of the country were eventually controlled by Carranza. However, Villa still attempted a military adventure in Sonora, where he was again defeated at Agua Prieta, Hermosillo, and other places; finally returning to the State of Chihuahua not as the powerful leader of the Northern Division but as a guerrilla leader who would cause serious problems to the Government —national as well as international.

Since he wanted to consolidate his government, Carranza decided to tour the northern part of the country; there on October 19 in the city of Torreón, he received an unexpected message: Wilson's Government recognized the

Government of the Revolution. The telegram sent to him in Torreón, read:

"Washington, D. C., October 19, 1915. Mr. V. Carranza, Torreón, Coahuila. The note which I received today from Mr. Robert Lansing, Secretary of State of the United States Government, is textually transcribed as follows:

'Dear Mr. Arredondo. I have the pleasure of informing you that the President of the United States takes this opportunity to extend his recognition of the de facto Government of Mexico, in which Mr. Don Venustiano Carranza functions as Chief Executive. The Government of the United States will be pleased to formally receive in Washington the diplomatic representative of said de facto Government as soon as Mr. Carranza wishes to name him and accredit his appointment; and reciprocally the Government of the United States will accredit before the de facto Government a diplomatic representative as soon as our President can duly appoint him. I would appreciate it if you would give this information to Mr. Carranza as soon as you deem it possible and opportune. I am, yours sincerely, R. Lansing.' "

Mr. Arredondo informed Carranza that he had received similar notes from the governments of Argentina, Brazil and Chile.

With these recognitions the Government of Mr. Carranza had attained the international support which was so important and so necessary. Little by little the Revolutionary Government was being consolidated. Recognition of Carranza by the United States made Villa deeply angry as he realized that his hated enemy would now have the support of the powerful United States, and that he, Villa, would not have the same considerations he previously had for the acquisition of arms and ammunition from this country. About that time Villa had again become the old guerrilla fighter which he had been at the beginning of his career. His horde of followers were unconditionally loyal to him, but against the United States. Two of these men, Pablo López and Rafael Castro, held up a train on January 10, 1916. Aboard travelled a group of Americans, employees of a mining company, American Smelting and Refining Company. The Villa band forced them out of the train and shot them for no apparent reason. Only Thomas H. Holmes, who was badly wounded, managed to escape and was able to tell what had happened. These murders took place at the train station of Santa Isabel. The Government of the United States presented a claim to Carranza's Government in the amount of $1,280,000 dollars for damages. From a legal standpoint, the Mexican Government did not accept this claim, although it recognized its moral justification. Nevertheless, the Constitutionalist Government declared Villa a fugitive from justice in the following Decree:

"Venustiano Carranza, Commander-in-Chief of the Constitutionalist Army and Commissioner of Executive Power of the Union, exercising the special rights conferred upon him, and considering:

"That the frequency with which the assaults being perpetrated by the gangs of bandits who are dispersed in several places within the country, after the Constitutionalist Army's annihiliation of armed resistance, calls for strong repressive measures and severe punishment of the parties responsible for such crimes, and in view of the last crime committed by the outlaws whose leaders are Guerrillas Rafael Castro and Pablo López, belonging to the forces of Francisco Villa from whom they get their orders, in which

*A typical scene of the Revolution. A group of "rurals" shipping their horses before leaving for a campaign.*

they held up a passenger train at a point eight kilometers to the west of Santa Isabel, State of Chihuahua and killed 18 Americans, and in accordance with the precedent established by the Constitutionalist Government for similar cases previously recorded, I have deemed it necessary to issue:

Article First. The reactionary guerrilla leader ex-General Francisco Villa is outlawed.

Article Second. The reactionaries ex-General Rafael Castro and ex-Colonel Pablo López, are outlawed.

Article Third. Any citizen of the Republic is herein authorized to arrest the rebel leaders Francisco Villa, Rafael Castro and Pablo López and execute them without trial, issuing a notorial certificate testifying to their identification and execution.

"Drawn up in the city of Querétaro on the fourteenth of January, nineteen sixteen. V. Carranza."

Two months later, another incident would occur which was much more serious than this one. On the night of March 9, Francisco Villa and a group of his followers attacked the small town of Columbus, New Mexico. In the holdup three soldiers and five civilians were killed, and seven soldiers were wounded. Several stores and private homes were robbed and burned. Two hours later the Villa band recrossed the border into Mexico. The excuse given for this incident was the refusal of a Jew named Rafael to give back money given to him by the Villa band for the purchase of ammunition.

This incident caused a big scandal in both countries. In the United States some of the press asked for a declaration of war against Mexico, others wanted Villa's head. The United States Government sent the Constitutionalist Government a note through its representative, Silliman, which stated "It seems that the present situation is the most serious one suffered by our government during the entire period of disturbances in Mexico, and we expect that the Mexican government will do everything in its power to pursue, capture and eliminate this gang which is now riding to the west of Columbus."

Mr. Carranza replied the following to the Secretary of State:

"Remembering the preceding events (attacks of red-skinned Indians in both countries) and the good results which the agreement referred to brought to both countries, this Government, presided over by the Chief Executive, wishing the elimination at the earliest possible moment of the horde headed by Francisco Villa. . . addresses itself to the Government of the United States requesting the necessary permission to enable Mexican forces to enter American Territory in pursuit of these bandits, granting the necessary reciprocity to the United States forces to enter into Mexican Territory in case the Columbus incident is unfortunately repeated at any other point along the border."

The Government of the United States took advantage of this note and ordered General John J. Pershing to enter Mexico. This command initiated the Punitive Expedition.

This regrettable incident occurred because of Villa's uncompromising attitude, his impulsiveness and hatred, and because the United States had misinterpreted the Mexican note in which it was clearly stated that entry could be made only if the attack was repeated; this did not occur.

The United States troops commanded by General Pershing were composed of the First Brigade, commanded by Colonel James Lockett, the Second Brigade, commanded by Colonel John J. Beacon, in addition to the necessary logistic services, making a total of 6,000 men.

This contingent was later reinforced, thereby increasing the amount of men.

General Pershing had precise instructions from his government to respect Mexican sovereignty. On its part, the State Department sent another note addressed to Mr. Carranza in similar terms. Upon learning of the entry into Mexico by the foreign force, the Mexican Government, in order to avoid further trouble, sent orders to the leaders of the Constitutionalist Army informing them of its diplomatic efforts and telling them to position their troops at convenient points in order to prevent any invasion of National Territory by American soldiers.

While American troops searched fruitlessly for Pancho Villa in Chihuahua, both governments initiated a series of diplomatic exchanges which were also futile. In addition, the Mexican Government sent serious warnings stating that American troops should not go deeper into the south of Mexico, as an armed clash could take place with Mexican troops. In spite of these warnings, on June 18 General Pershing ordered Captain Boyd who, with a section of troops of the Tenth Cavalry Regiment, marched to the Hacienda of Santo Domingo, situated on the outskirts of the town of El Carrizal, with the purpose of joining the column of Captain S. Morey. Soldiers of the Second Cavalry Regiment of the Canales Brigade were stationed near El Carrizal; they were commanded by Lieutenant Colonel Genovevo Rivas Guillén. This troop was to join the First Regiment, all of which would then be under the command of General Félix U. Gómez, totalling some 300 soldiers.

On the morning of June 21, the Mexican soldiers observed the advance of the American soldiers. General Gómez was informed of this and ordered Lieutenant Colonel

Rivas to talk to the American officers. The interview was not successful since the American commander ordered his troops to advance. Upon seeing this, General Gómez ordered the bugler to sound "fire". A skirmish ensued in which the Mexican general was killed. A short time afterwards Captain Boyd and Lieutenant Adair met the same fate. This skirmish only served to sharpen the differences between the two governments, which again met at New London to try to find a solution. These meetings were continued in Atlantic City and adjourned on November 24, 1916, when a treaty was signed whereby the Punitive Expedition would abandon Mexican Territory. This was not done until February 6, 1917, when General Pershing returned to his country without completing his mission.

Thus ended this irritating chapter for both countries, which had stretched the relations between them to the breaking point at a time when a reconciliation was so necessary, especially because of the threatening predictions in Europe of a war with the United States.

To bring this chapter to a close, we shall comment a bit on a few laws of a social nature which were published by the revolutionaries. One of these laws was published by General Obregón in which minimum wages were established for the States of Michoacán, Querétaro, Hidalgo and Guanajuato; country laborers as well as city laborers were included in this law. This decree was ratified by Carranza and it was noted that it would be extended to the degree to which the constitutionalist government might extend its control to the rest of the Republic.

Pancho Villa was not left behind in this matter as, in spite of the fact that he never had brilliant social ideologies, he was advised to publish a provision, agrarian in nature, in order to gain the support of the farmers. He did so on

January 6, 1915, when he published a law in the *Gaceta Oficial* (Official Gazette) of the State Government of Chihuahua. This land reform law was never enforced. About this time in far-away Yucatán the First Feminist Congress was being held as a result of the summons issued by General Alvarado, Governor and Military Commander of that state.

In Veracruz a Congress of Workers was held and a declaration of principles was approved, thereby constituting the Confederation of Workers of the Mexican Region. This congress was important because the precepts of class struggle, socialization of the means of production and the use of direct action as a tactic in the struggle were accepted; in other words, the principles and tactics of international socialism.

*An unusual photograph of revolutionaries
upon proclamation of the
Plan of Agua Prieta, 1920.*

# 8

Venustiano Carranza calls a Constituent Congress. The Constitution of 1917. Citizen Venustiano Carranza is elected President of the Republic. The Carranza Goverment.

Even though Mr. Carranza had named his movement Constitutionalist because he had raised the flag of legality in representation of the Constitution of 1857, which had been violated by Huerta, in the course of the struggle ideologies and long-suppressed wishes surged in the Mexican people. There were important ideological groups influenced by the great currents of socialism, communism to a lesser degree, and some who followed the anarchist current, although much fewer in number. The foremost problem was agrarian; Zapata had adopted it as his own and had proclaimed it in the Plan of Ayala. There were the great latifundia to the north of the Republic, and, in a prominent place were the dreams, dissatisfactions and the millenary injustices which had been perpetrated against millions of farmers who did not possess even the piece of land on which they lived. The laborers, a small stratum, but who were class-conscious and demanded a dignified place in the new Mexican society, had also paid their dues in blood as they had organized and sent to the front the Workers' Battalions. There was also a middle class, intelligent and competitive, which did not want and would not accept the privileges enjoyed by the Porfirian pseudo-aristocracy. All these currents, although disjointed, fought to become united and give Mexico a new social order. Hence, groups began to appear which proclaimed, at first timidly and then openly, the need of reforming the Constitution of 1857. Still other groups fought for the creation of a new Magna Carta which would gather together the hopes, dreams and needs of the Mexican people. Much blood had been spilled and everyone was conscious of the need of ending secular privileges, of creating a new democracy which would sweep away the hateful system of "caciquismo" (bossism). Everyone hoped that the slogan "Effective Suffrage, No Reelection", created by Madero to initiate the revolution against the old caudillo, would come true.

In addition, in the new army were a few figures with progressive ideas, like Francisco J. Múgica, Heriberto Jara, Esteban Baca Calderón; civilians like Luis G. Monzón, Luis Manuel Rojas and Juan de Dios Bojórquez. These people did not propose changes in the Constitution of 1857 —they simply wanted a new constitution.

Don Venustiano Carranza was aware of this grave restlessness, but was unable to remedy it until he had ended the civil strife instigated by the rupture in the

Revolution. However, because of the battles of Celaya, León, Aguascalientes, etc., where the Villa movement had finally been stamped out, the situation was becoming clear and the time was approaching when these arduous problems would be resolved. At the time of the Revolution when he was reforming and adding to the Plan of Guadalupe, Mr. Carranza had already made known his willingness to enact new laws of a social nature. When he had made these reforms he had said: "The Commander of the Revolution will issue and enforce during the struggle all the laws, provisions and measures channeled to satisfying the economic, social and political needs of the country, bringing about the reforms which public opinion demands as essential for the reestablishment of the regime which will guarantee equality to all Mexicans."

We should recall the Law of January 6, 1915, clearly social in nature, by which the alienation of communal lands belonging to natives is declared null and void; likewise, settlements, concessions and sales made by tax autorities are declared null and void.

Another clear indication of his desire to draw up a new constitution is found in the telegram sent by Carranza to his collaborator, Eliseo Arredondo in Washington, in which he says: "When peace is again attained, I shall call a Congress, duly elected by popular vote of all citizens, which will be constituent in character, in order to elevate the reforms dictated during the struggle to constitutional precepts."

Finally, on September 14, 1916, the Decree reforming Articles Fourth, Fifth and Sixth of the Plan of Guadalupe, was published and a Constituent Congress was called in which it was hoped that "the entire nation would indubitably exercise the act of will because in this way, while all questions which have been requiring solution would be fully discussed and resolved in the best possible way in order to satisfy public needs, we would also achieve in a relatively short time the introduction of a legal system on a solid basis and under such legitimate conditions that no one would dare to oppose them." On September 19th the notice of the Constituents' Meeting was published as a preliminary step before calling the Constituent Congress into session. In Article First, the Mexican people were called to elect deputies for Congress, who would meet in the city of Querétaro commencing December 1. Elections were held and approximately 200 deputies gathered in this city which was the cradle of the Constitution.

The brand new deputies enthusiastically assembled in Querétaro where political parties were formed which had already been taking shape according to their ideological convictions, such as liberals, renovators, etc. Activities began with eleven preliminary meetings. The deputies were a multifarious group who represented the most diversified social classes of the Mexican nation. Of course, there was an important group of military men, or "armed citizens" as they were then called; there were attorneys, engineers, a few newspapermen, farmers, etc.

The Congress already in session began holding its important and dramatic meeting on December 1, 1916. Let us see how it is described by an eye-witness and actual survivor. He is Don Jesús Romero Flores, historian and teacher, who tells us:

"The Chamber of Deputies was richly decorated. Placed at the rear was the directors' platform; the orators' rostrum was located at the end of the forum as were tables for parliamentary stenographers; curule chairs for the deputies were arranged throughout the chamber; the pit contained the seats assigned to the diplomatic corps; the balconies were bursting with an enormous audience from all social classes; the common people attended in greater numbers —there were farmers and workers from the factories located on the outskirts of Querétaro, all of whom occupied the balconies and galleries.

"Mr. Carranza sat in the place of honor on the platform with the president of the Congress at his right, and occupying the remaining seats were the members of the board of directors, the secretaries of State and General Federico Montes, Governor of Querétaro.

"Attorney Rojas, breaking the silence enveloping the chamber, declared:

'The Constituent Congress convenes this first day of December nineteen sixteen, its sole period of sessions.'

"Then Mr. Carranza began reading his address which was listened to attentively, and in which he made a judicious analysis of the Constitution of 1857 which would be reformed; of the underlying reasons for the reforms; and finally, of the articles which to his judgment should be amended. He put the Project of Reforms into the hands of the president of the Congress, submitting it for study and deliberation by the assembly."

To many deputies the Project of Reforms seemed too moderate and the group constituting what could be called leftwing, opposed it.

New projects were proposed and discussed heatedly, and thus were derived Articles Third, 27th, 28th, 123rd and 130th which are of the greatest political and social significance.

The article which provoked the most discussion and which, to the present time, is one of the most attacked, is Article Third which refers to education. It decrees that "instruction is free, but that which is imparted in official institutions of learning will be secular and not religious; this also applies to elementary or higher education imparted in private institutions."

It was decreed that: "No religious society or minister of any cult, can establish or direct schools of elementary education," that "private elementary schools can only be established under official surveillance," and finally, that "in official institutions elementary education will be imparted free of charge." This article was later amended but in its time it was considered a very important social advance.

The above-mentioned article which established secular instruction, that is, non-religious in nature, was completed by Article 130 which confirmed the separation of State and Church. The essence of the article is as follows:

"The federal powers have the exclusive right to intervene with regard to religious cults and external discipline, as set forth by the law. The State and Church are independent of each other. Congress cannot make laws establishing or prohibiting any religion. . ."

The other two articles which provoked heated debates and long discussions for their approval, were the 27th and 123rd. The leftist group fought most vigorously for their approval. Article 27th stipulates that land and water are national property and that the nation has the power of imposing the legal formalities which public interest might dictate. Another very important point referred to expropriation for public use and was complemented with the clear-cut affirmation that the Nation was the owner of subsoil resources and that this control was inalienable and imprescriptible. Here was the legal basis which in later years would make the expropriation of petroleum feasible.

It was done in 1938. Thus this group of foresighted men made possible the recovery of Mexico's petroleum from foreign hands.

This same article also became the legal basis for land reforms, a matter of vital importance to Mexico. The preliminary discussions brought out the fact that nearly three million peons did not possess any land, while 11,000 landowners were the proprietors of two-thirds of the national territory, of which 834 possessed 1,300,000 square kilometers. Almost two-thirds of the Republic!

Article 27th was adopted; today it constitutes the basis for Agrarian Reform, and is one of the most advanced from a social standpoint. In addition to paving the way for the expropriation of petroleum, it contributed to strengthening the economic independence of Mexico by assuring another type of riches for the country —sulphur, uranium, etc.

Article 23rd was also quite advanced in a social sense: it set up relations between workers and employees as well as the foundation for more humane and equitable labor conditions.

The constituent deputies who took a major part in carefully working out and drawing up the aforementioned article were Attorney José N. Macías, Engineer Pastor Rouaix, Deputy Rafael L. de los Ríos, in addition to the valuable assistance and influence given by Attorney Andrés Molina Enríquez.

Article 23rd set up standards for minimum wages, an eight-hour work-day and working conditions for minors. Undoubtedly this was one of the great social achievements of those years.

The constitution had been completed satisfactorily and February 5 was designated for its proclamation. In the closing session, Attorney Luis Manuel Rojas, while delivering a speech, addressed Mr. Carranza in the following terms:

"If in a few points we have gone a little beyond what your wisdom has indicated as a just and prudent middle-of-the-road policy regarding the opposing national tendencies, the glow of youth, which has followed our glorious flag raised on high by you in Guadalupe, your revolutionary enthusiasm after the struggle, and your natural eagerness to break away from old social patterns, in this way reacting against inveterate vices of the past, might explain sufficiently the motives within the hearts of the members of this Assembly in straying somewhat from the serene and perfectly justifiable path which you have traced for us. . ."

"From any viewpoint, it is clear that the legislation emerging from this Congress as an outstanding point of admiration of the great Constitutionalist Revolution, should be characterized by its tendency to look for new horizons and to set aside the hallowed concepts of yesteryear for the benefit of the populace which makes up the majority of the Mexican people, who have been traditionally disinherited and oppressed."

The new Constitution was solemnly proclaimed on February 5. Mexico now had a new law which gave it confidence for a greater well-being. On February 6 the people were called upon for presidential, senatorial and deputy elections corresponding to the next constitutional term. The elections were held on March 11, and the man who had led the Mexican people to victory was elected. Citizen Venustiano Carranza Garza became President of the Republic. On April 15 the new Congress was convened, and on May 1 the old Commander-in-Chief of the Constitutionalist

Army and Commissioner of Executive Power, assumed the Presidency. Mexico had entered the road to legality.

The first constitutionalist cabinet was integrated in the following manner: Attorney Ernesto Garza Pérez (Undersecretary) in charge of the Office in Foreign Affairs; Attorney Manuel Aguirre Berlanga (Undersecretary) in the Interior; Rafael Nieto (Undersecretary) in the Treasury; General Jesús Agustín Castro (Undersecretary) in War and the Navy; Manuel Rodríguez Gutiérrez (Undersecretary) in Communications; Engineer Pastor Rouaix in Development; Engineer Alberto J. Pani in Industry and Commerce; Doctor-General José Siurob in the Department of Health; General César López de Lara as Governor of the Federal District. The Judicial Power was composed of Ministers Enrique M. de los Ríos, Enrique Colunga, Victoriano Pimentel, Agustín del Valle, Enrique García Parra, Manuel E. Cruz, Enrique Moreno, Santiago Martínez Alomía, José M. Trechuelo, Alberto González and Agustín Urdapilleta.

General Alvaro Obregón, who had been Secretary of War and the Navy, resigned his post saying that his services were no longer needed and he retired to his native Sonora to await the development of events. There, like a modern Cincinnatus, he would dedicate himself to farming.

In these months elections were held for State governors. As was logical, a goodly number of generals were elected, as they were the conquerors of the Revolution. In Jalisco, General Manuel M. Diéguez, famous since the strike in Cananea, and who would be shot and killed in the de la Huerta rebellion, was elected governor; in Veracruz, General Cándido Aguilar, who was the son-in-law of Mr. Carranza and an old revolutionary, was elected governor; in Hidalgo, General Nicolás Flores; in Campeche, General

Joaquín Mucel; in Sinaloa, General Ramón F. Iturbe, another old revolutionary from the Madero era; in Sonora, General Plutarco Elías Calles, a future president of the Republic; in Zacatecas, General Enrique Estrada; in Guerrero, General Silvestre Mariscal; in Durango, General Domingo Arrieta, also an old revolutionary; in Michoacán, Engineer-General Pascual Ortiz Rubio, also a future president of the Republic.

Unfortunately, the country was a long way from peace, in spite of Carranza's conciliatory efforts: bands of Villa, Zapata and Félix Díaz followers wandered in the states of Chihuahua, Morelos and Veracruz. Zapata, the eternal rebel, controlled almost all the state of Morelos because only the principal cities of that state were in the hands of the government. Félix Díaz had returned to the country and was operating from Veracruz and the Istmus of Tehuantepec; he even had partisans in far-away Chiapas. In the important region of the Huastecas, a petroleum zone par excellence, General Manuel Peláez, who was closely linked to foreign petroleum companies, was in control. Carranza realized that in order to annihilate these rebel groups, it would be necessary to reorganize the constitutionalist army and give it a professional character. Consequently, he decreed the creation of a school which would train future officers for the new army. With this purpose in mind, investigations, diverse plans and deliberations were initiated, which would be the basis for the new educational institution of the Revolution.

On July 20, 1916, these projects became a reality since on that day, the Academia del Estado Mayor (Military Staff Academy) came into being, destined to carry out the mission of "imparting the related instruction until such time as the necessary buildings are established and instruction will be broader."

The inauguration took place on October 20th of that year, presided over by Mr. Carranza and Generals Alvaro Obregón, Benjamín Hill, Francisco L. Urquizo, and others. Engineer Angel Vallejo, a veteran general who had belonged to the extinct Federal Army, was appointed as its first director.

This military academy ceased to exist on December 31, 1919, since the Military School was about to reopen its doors.

Another educational military institution which was established in those days was the Constitutionalist Military Medical School, which was founded on January 1, 1917, thanks to the efforts of Military Doctors Enrique Osorno and Guadalupe García García, and with the aid of a select group of military doctors who put their full attention and collaboration to the creation of this school.

Another important occurrence at this time was the impulse given to the establishment of a military industry; the difficulties regarding the acquisition of arms and ammunition from abroad, principally from the United States, were well known.

In his book *Carranza's Legacy,* Attorney Cabrera stated some interesting ideas in this respect, which, in part, are as follows:

"It was not that he was unaware that war materials could be gotten in sufficient amounts and cheaper by buying them in the United States, which had been the main supplier of arms and equipment for the past ten years. However, in his desire for autonomy he did not want us to continue being the possible victims of an arms embargo and then having the embargo lifted. . ."

"Please understand clearly that the problem of manufacturing arms and equipment is not for international ends but because of an autonomous tendency: the solution of our military problems was not in our hands, but in those of the individuals who sold us, or did not sell us, the indispensable supplies for attaining peace. What Carranza always sought when he tried to get military supplies for Mexico was precisely what he sought in international spheres: the nonintervention or influence of foreign nations in our internal affairs."

As a consequence, these efforts resulted in the creation of military factories which began to make the necessary arms and ammunition to satisfy the needs of the Army.

The year 1919 would be important as transcendental events would occur. The first of these was the death of the southern leader, Emiliano Zapata, who, as we have seen, refused to be under the control of any of the preceding governments, much less that of Carranza's, which he did not recognize. In the early part of that year, he addressed a letter to President Carranza, written in very harsh terms, which said:

"No one believes in you any longer, or in your talent as a pacifier, or in your stature as a politician and governor. . . It is time for you to step down, it is time to leave the post to men who are more capable and more honorable. It would be a crime to prolong this situation of an undeniable moral, economic and political bankruptcy. . . Your staying in power is an obstacle to initiating the work of union and reconstruction. Because of your intransigent attitude and the mistakes you have made, progressive men who act in good faith have been made useless in collaborating with your government, men who could have been useful to Mexico. . . These men, these intellectuals, this youth, full of ideals, these new people, unstained, uncorrupted or spent, these revolutionaries of yesteryear, have cut themselves off from public affairs full of disenchantment; these youths who have begun with great principles of the Revolution and anxiously feel deeply about fulfilling them, these lovers of ideals, who today have filled their souls with longing for an honorable and strong government, driven with generous longings and anxious to meet the obligations contracted in a solemn hour."

"However, for the sake of duty and honor, in the name of humanity and patriotism, resign from the high post which today you occupy and from which you have caused the ruin of the country."

This letter, although exaggerated, described the situation of unrest, and, above all, it opened up in Morelos a possible center of insurrection. Mr. Carranza, accordingly, ordered General Pablo González to intensify his operations against Zapata. General González made plans to eliminate the southern caudillo by means of an ambush. To carry out this plan, González counted on one of his staunchest leaders, Colonel Jesús Guajardo, who, pretending to be at odds with the government, made known his wishes to go over to the Zapata rank and file. This astute colonel was able to convince Zapata of his discontent, even though Zapata never trusted anyone. Zapata wrote a letter to his future assassin in which he says: "With us you will contribute to the triumph of the great revolutionary cause which strives for the good of the humble classes, and when we have become victorious, you will have the satisfaction of having fulfilled your duty and your conscious will be at peace for having acted with justice."

Guajardo coaxed Zapata to go to the Chinameca Hacienda where the colonel's regiment was stationed. Not suspecting the end which awaited him, Zapata did just this. He reached the former hacienda on April 10th and as he was approaching the old, battered door, the sentinels, who apparently started to present arms in his honor, opened fire on him and his escort. Zapata fell to the ground, riddled with bullets. Thus fell the legendary figure of the agrarian reform.

The corpse was taken to the neighboring town of Cuautla, where it was exposed to the curiosity of the populace. Colonel Guajardo was promoted for his feat and, in addition, received a prize of $50,000 pesos.

Meanwhile, the political situation worsened. General Obregón, an unquestionable military and political figure, had expressed his desire of becoming a candidate for the presidential elections, but Carranza had picked out as the official candidate Engineer Ignacio Bonillas, a man of honor but completely obscure, with no political background and, of course, totally insignificant in comparison to Obregón.

In the same year of 1919, another drama of the many written during the Revolution, was taking place in Chihuahua. General Felipe Angeles had returned to Mexico from the United States. He had encountered Villa but on this occasion he could not exert the influence which he had had so long ago, nor could he organize the Villa troops. They had lost their character as an organized force and had become guerrilla bands. Disappointed, Angeles severed his relations with Villa and became independent. He could do nothing, however, as he lacked the overwhelming popularity of the other caudillos of the Revolution. In spite of this, he was feared and hated by Carranza because of his intelligence and the influence he had enjoyed with the Northern Division. It was said that Angeles had played a significant role in causing the rupture in the Revolution. The Government put a price on his head when it became aware that he had returned to the state of Chihuahua. He enjoyed his freedom for a very short time —on November 15th he was taken prisoner at a place known as Valle de los Olivos, near Parral. The prisoners were then transferred to the capital of the State where they arrived on the afternoon of the 21st.

During the trip and later in prison, General Angeles showed himself to be, as he in reality was, a superior being who was very different from the mediocrities surrounding him. He was taken to the barracks of the 21st Cavalry Regiment, where he was incarcerated to await court-martial. In this regard, General Diéguez received a telegram from the President of the Republic, Mr. Carranza, saying: "General D. Manuel Diéguez. Chihuahua. I have been advised of the formation of a Court-Martial who will try Felipe Angeles. Enforce the law to its utmost, without permitting influences of any kind in favor or against the accused. Affectionate greetings. V. Carranza."

In the first days of his captivity, it was thought that Angeles would not be shot, but when word got around that he would be court-martialed, everyone realized that his fate was sealed. The principal newspapers in Chihuahua published the news, informing everyone that the trial would be held at the Teatro de los Héroes (Heroes' Theater).

Attorney Leandro Díaz de León was appointed trial judge and he immediately went to take the statements from the accused, who, besides Angeles, were Major Arce and a young man named Antonio Trillo. On the night of the 22nd, the accused designated their legal counsel,

Attorneys Alberto López Hermosa and Alfonso Gómez Luna, who immediately requested constitutional guarantee for protection of their civil rights from the Supreme Court of Justice of the Republic, in order to have the court-martial suspended. However, suspension was denied by the military authorities. In consequence, a Special Court-Martial was called and the trial would begin on Monday, the 24th. That day a crowd assembled at the theater since everybody wanted to witness the trial of the famous revolutionary general.

The Council was comprised of (President) General Gabriel Gavira, (Members) Brigadier Generals Miguel M. Acosta, Fernando Peraldi, Silvino M. García and José Gonzalo Escobar (who would lead an uprising in 1929). The trial judge was Attorney and General Leandro M. Díaz de León; (consultant attorney) General Víctor Prieto and (counsel for the defense) Attorney Alfonso Gómez Luna.

From the start the defense lawyers alleged that the Court-Martial could not try Angeles as a military man as he was in fact no longer a general because he was not listed in the army register and therefore could not be tried for the offense of rebellion. All the efforts of the defense failed, including the judicial proceedings made in the capital of the Republic. The Court-Martial completed its deliberations and sentenced ex-General Felipe Angeles to death. Ex-Major Arce was also sentenced to death although his sentence was later commuted to 20 years in prison. Private Trillo was condemned to eight years in prison.

According to an eye-witness, General Angeles heard the sentence with absolute calm. His face did not reveal the slightest trace of nervousness.

Angeles's last hours were serene; he devoted himself to writing to his wife (who was in New York at the time) and to putting down on paper a few thoughts.

On the morning of November 27, 1919, at 6:00 a.m., the sentence was executed. A description of these last dramatic moments is contained in the book on Felipe Angeles written by Engineer Cervantes. He says:

"The scene was poignant. The pale daylight hardly illuminated the small room in which General Angeles was sitting, by now surrounded by many people who, silently, trembling with emotion, stared at the prisoner who so calmly awaited the signal to confront his executioners.

"No one ventured to break the silence which prevailed. Outside the little room could be heard the steps of soldiers and officers ordering: 'To the right, line up!'

"At a signal from Major Campos, Angeles quickly got up from his chair, threw the blanket which had kept him warm onto the bed, and firmly embracing Attorney Gómez Luna said in a loud voice that he was taking leave of those present and would pray for the re-establishment of peace in the Republic.

"Then roughly he hurried toward the place of execution. He had just put himself in front of the firing squad commanded by Lieutenant Ramón Ortiz, when Ortiz's voice was heard ordering: 'Fire.' and a unisonous volley pierced the air.

"The body of General Angeles rolled to the left, partly flexed, with an arm under his head and the stertorous sounds of the agony of dying were heard, until one of the soldiers of the escort administered the death blow by a bullet in the head, terminating the existence of this man who was a glory to our National Army."

The life of General Felipe Angeles had come to an end; one of the most outstanding and controversial figures of the Mexican Revolution, which implacably devoured its most faithful exponents.

Let us return now to the political struggle which would culminate in the elimination of one of its principal figures. As we have said before, General Obregón was determined to be one of the candidates for presidency of the Republic, in opposition to Carranza's candidate, Engineer Bonillas. The political fields had not been perfectly defined, but little by little they were becoming clear. In Carranza's cabinet, General Plutarco Elías Calles, figured as Minister of Industry and Commerce. He was a native of Sonora and faithful to General Obregón; therefore, he did not hesitate to present his resignation in order to return to his home State. This action made Carranza realize the imminence of the struggle. Referring to Calles' resignation, Carranza said: "I am deeply concerned with the resignation of General Calles from my cabinet, as I feel a profound esteem for him and, in addition to this, I consider him a true patriot and irreproachable revolutionary. To the present time he has been a loyal and sincere collaborator in my government and I am quite sure that if some day the country and the revolution are in danger, Calles will be the man who will save them."

The electoral campaign was launched: General Obregón and General González against Bonillas.

Obregón initiated his political campaign by touring the Republic and, as was to be expected, he found the country riddled with problems and incidents like the one that ocurred in Tampico in which a group of those close to him suffered abuses at the hands of the military commander. While he was in Matamoros, Obregón received a telegram from General Urquizo in charge of the Ministry of War, advising him to return to Mexico City because the President of the Republic had ordered a judge to start legal action against him for the offense of rebellion, since there was suspicion of a relationship between him and General Roberto Cejudo, a Félix Díaz follower up in arms against the government.

General Obregón departed for Mexico City where he was watched closely.

From Sonora, Calles made known his intentions in a letter addressed to Attorney Zubarán in which he tells him the following:

"All the people of the State have become aware of the criminal plans of Carranza and they are ready to the man to defend peace and support their government... I am willing to sacrifice my life in order to establish the principle of forbidding new dictatorships in Mexico."

Meantime, many leaders began joining the Sonora leaders such as Roberto Cruz, Colonel Abelardo L. Rodríguez, Colonel Topete, General Jesús M. Aguirre, and many others.

Because of the events occurring in Mexico, Adolfo de la Huerta, Governor of the State, appointed General Calles military Commander of the State so that "he might as a matter of course assume the command of all military forces within that entity and proceed to prepare the defense of the sovereignty of said State." This was a tacit declaration of war. Soon afterwards the local legislature broke ties with the Central Government. Steps were taken to activate enlistment.

On April 12 hostilities were openly declared when de la Huerta appointed Calles Supreme Chief of the First Division Corps of the Northeastern Army, with orders to march to the south and combat the Carranza troops who would disembark in Mazatlán. General Cruz and General Flores received orders to the same effect.

The rebellion started spreading: General Iturbe surrendered in Culiacán; General Arnulfo R. Gómez (who would attempt an uprising in 1927) surrendered in Tampico; Michoacán, Morelos, Tamaulipas, Tabasco, Campeche and Veracruz also joined the movement. Enrique Estrada in Zacatecas disavowed Carranza. The designation of a name and the development of a plan for the movement were the only items left to do. However, the small city of Agua Prieta would be the one to baptize the new revolutionary movement, which we intend to analyze in the next chapter.

To close the present chapter, we have left until last a very interesting episode which occurred in these years and which had an international transcendency, even greater than within the Republic. We refer to the famous Zimmermann telegram which played quite an important role in making the United States abandon its policy of neutrality and enter into the First World War on the side of the allies.

Briefly, the story is the following:

The German Minister of Foreign Affairs, Arthur Zimmermann, thought up the possibility of offering an offensive-defensive alliance to Mexico. He broached the subject to Kaiser William II and obtained his approval. The instructions would reach the German ambassador in Mexico, von Eckhardt, through the German ambassador in the United States, Count Albert von Bernstorff, as this round-about way was considered safe. Zimmermann sent the following instructions to Bernstorff, carrying out their plan:

"Absolutely confidential. For the personal information of his Excellency and to be transmitted to the imperial minister of Mexico by a safe route." Then came the famous message to Eckhardt, which said:

"We want to begin the submarine war without restrictions on February Ist. In spite of this, we shall try to keep the United States neutral; in case neutrality is not achieved, we propose an alliance with Mexico on the following points: to carry out a war together, a generous financial support, and agreement on our part that Mexico recover her lost territories in Texas, New Mexico and Arizona. Agreement on details will be left to his Excellency. You will inform the President (of Mexico) in absolute secrecy of what is happening as soon as entry by the United States in the War is confirmed and you will add the suggestion that he, on his own initiative, invite Japan and, at the same time, become a mediator between Japan and us.

"Please call the President's attention to the fact that the use, without restrictions, of our submarines offers the opportunity of coercing England to sign peace within a few months. I acknowledge receipt."

*ZIMMERMANN"*

This telegram was intercepted by Chamber 40 of English Naval Counter-Espionage under the orders of Admiral Reginald Hall, and was immediately forwarded to Washington where it caused great commotion. Soon Ambassador Bernstorff left the United States and that country then joined the war on the side of the allies. In Mexico, Mr. Carranza handled the matter with great diplomatic ability, refusing to enter a dubious alliance which perhaps would have gravely compromised the integrity of Mexico. The Germans had thought that, taking into consideration that there were more than 100,000 armed men in our country, this could have caused a serious problem to the United States and could have made the mobilization of troops slower, giving them the necessary time for Germany to deliver the decisive blow to the weakened allies in Europe. However, Carranza adamantly refused and avoided entering into an alliance which would possibly have created another international conflict.

# 9

Obregón disavows Carranza. The Plan of Agua Prieta. Venustiano Carranza leaves Mexico City. Tlaxcalantongo. May 1920. The death of President Carranza. Transitional Government of Don Adolfo de la Huerta. The Government of Alvaro Obregón comes to power.

Let us see now what the political situation was in those frenetic months of the first half of 1920.

Carranza had made a decision that would be fatal to him: his candidate for President of the Republic was to be Engineer Ignacio Bonillas, Ambassador to the United States. We have already stated that Mr. Bonillas was practically unknown in political circles and no rival for Pablo González, and very much less for Obregón.

The formal political campaign was initiated in January. On the 18th the government newspaper *The Democrat* published a manifesto of the Democratic National Party formally announcing Bonillas as candidate. In February there was a meeting in the capital of seventeen governors, convened by Carranza to discuss the future elections; a manifesto was published in which the political conditions of the country were detailed; they abstained from backing any particular candidate and stated that they would do everything in their power to guarantee an honest election. They also hinted at the possibility of a rebellion. The *Republican Monitor,* a newspaper which backed Obregón, denied the possibility of any uprising. Obregón's supporters also held a meeting in Mexico. Among them were well-known figures such as General Benjamín Hill, the Yucatecan leader Felipe Carrillo Puerto, Attorney Miguel Alessio Robles, and others. These men prepared an 18-point program among which were free election, no reelection, local and state autonomy, etc.

The situation came to a crisis in Sonora, where Adolfo de la Huerta, a well-known revolutionary figure, governed. Carranza, with the pretext of placating the Yaqui tribe, decided to dispatch General Manuel M. Diéguez, but his real intention was to replace de la Huerta. The latter, realizing Carranza's intentions, initiated an interchange of messages with the President.

By the month of April, the situation had become very tense because Carranza insisted on sending federal soldiers to Sonora which de la Huerta was violently opposed to; in a telegram sent on April 7th, the Governor requested information as to the Central Government's intentions. Carranza replied that "he would not discuss with a state government the convenience or inconvenience of military movements dictated within the constitutional powers accorded him." On April 8th Calles sent a telegram to Diéguez advising that he should not mobilize his troops to the State, under penalty that this would constitute the initiation of a civil war. Finally, after Calles was named Commander of the First Division of the Northwestern Corps of the Army by de la Huerta, his mission being to prevent federal forces from landing in Mazatlán, the rupture with Carranza's government was clearly evident.

On April 23rd the entire situation was cleared up. In the tiny border town of Agua Prieta, Sonora, the Plan known by that name was signed which stated among other things: "Citizen Venustiano Carranza is hereby relieved of the exercise of the Executive Power of the Federation; the generals, official heads and soldiers who endorse this Plan shall constitute the Liberal Constitutionalist Army, the Supreme Commander of the Liberal Constitutionalist Army (de la Huerta) shall assume the Provisional Presidency of the Republic. . ." The Provisional President shall convoke elections for the Executive and Legislative powers of the Federation as soon as he assumes the duties of his office."

The above was signed among others by Plutarco Elías Calles, Abelardo L. Rodríguez, Fausto Topete, Luis L. León, José M. Tapia (Obregón's brother-in-law) Francisco R. Manzo, Alejandro Mange, Jesús M. Aguirre.

In the meantime, General Obregón was in the capital of the Republic subject to trial for trying to establish relations with General Roberto Cejudo, a Félix supporter. Obregón realized that he was lost in that city, because, in addition, he was subject to strict vigilance and he therefore planned his flight to the north. This he accomplished by means of a dramatic escape, leaving by train disguised as a railroad man with the help of Margarito Ramírez. The train left on April 12th at 5:30 p.m. in the evening and reached Iguala, Guerrero at 4:25.

The State of Guerrero was rife with Obregón supporters. One of the first to pledge his allegiance was General Rómulo Figueroa. From Iguala, they went to Coacoyula on horseback, pursued by General Fortunato Maycotte, who caught up with him in Venta Vieja. There, the following dialogue took place:

"What are you doing here, my General" asked Maycotte.

"Taking advantage of the guarantees which the Government offers honest men" replied Obregón. "How about you?" he added. "I've come here to arrest and execute you according to the orders I'm carrying. Come. Give me an ar," replied Maycotte. Obregón had saved himself. Later, in the company of Eduardo Neri and the future labor leader, Luis N. Morones, they headed for Chilpancingo, capital of the State. On the 20th of the month, the Government of Guerrero, disavowed President Carranza. In the remainder of the Republic the revolution raged uncontainably.

As Attorney Luis Cabrera put it, the "Strike of the Generals" had come to pass.

In the capital of the Republic, the Government was aware of the seriousness of the danger and secretly prepared to once again abandon the city. Very few military men remained loyal to the vacillating Carranza regime. Among them were Manuel M. Diéguez, Marciano González, the valiant Francisco Murguía, the Military Aviation School and the Military School which was at the point of writing another page of glorious defense of the dying regime. Mr. Carranza thought of taking refuge in the beautiful port of Veracruz, where he had once installed his government. Before leaving the capital, this time forever, Mr. Carranza had said:

"The only thing that will save us now is that it won't be long before Obregón and Pablo González are at loggerheads for the Presidency; then we shall decide the issue." Unfortunately for him, this prediction did not prove true, and a short time later he would be dead.

In the North, the rebel forces advanced irrevocably. In Chihuahua General Ignacio Enríquez, Governor of the State, informed de la Huerta at the beginning of May that the entire state had rebelled in favor of Obregón. . . that he, of course, would honor the Plan of Agua Prieta and stand by him along with Generals Eugenio Martínez, Joaquín Amaro, Alfredo Rueda Quijano, Abundio Gómez and José Amarillas.

Another General, Angel Flores, was marching against the port of Mazatlán, General Arnulfo R. Gómez (who a few years later would be shot on orders from Obregón when he rebelled in 1927) disavowed Carranza in Tamaulipas; Celestino Gasca did the same in Puebla and even Jacinto B. Treviño and Pablo González, who owed so much to Carranza, disavowed him and departed for Texcoco.

De la Huerta as Provisional President, named Calles Secretary of War and General Salvador Alvarado was designated Head of the Treasury Department. He also named several of his devoted followers governors of several federal entities, such as Paulino Guerrero in San Luis Potosí; Attorney Luis Sánchez Pontón in Puebla; Jesús Acevedo in Oaxaca; Attorney Emilio Portes Gil in Tamaulipas; and, as a logical result of the now imminent downfall of the Carranza government, numerous public officials and governors of the dying regime, such as Attorney Gustavo Espinoza Mireles of Coahuila, Severino Martínez of San Luis Potosí and General de los Santos of Nuevo León, began to abandon the city.

In Mexico City, Don Venustiano remained imperturbable, making plans, but he still wished to attend a last official act, the 5th of May celebration. However, it was no longer possible to remain in the threatened city and it was determined that May 7th was the day on which the city should be evacuated. Preparations were made which resulted excessive, because government employees, filing cabinets and the money in the Treasury could not be left behind, in addition to the eternal group of civilians and relatives who did not wish to abandon their loved ones in moments of danger.

The day of departure arrived and the enormous convoys began to move slowly out of the Buenavista and Colonia railroad stations. The departure took place in the midst of great confusion; only a few of the units were able to maintain order and discipline. Among these the most outstanding was the Military School which once again gave proof of its loyalty to the establishment.

They were hindered by one stop after another, making progress terribly slow. During the trip the convoy was shot at by groups of rebels.

In Apizaco, Tlaxcala, President Carranza reviewed his scanty forces: some were troops commanded by Generals Francisco Murguía, Lucio Blanco, Pilar R. Sánchez, Agustín Millán Millán, Federico Montes, Francisco de P. Mariel, Heliodoro Pérez, and others.

During the trip desertions increased, entire units went over to the rebels; commanders who only days before had pledged their loyalty to the President, now did not hesitate for a moment to jump on the victor's bandwagon, oblivious to their duties and their word of honor.

It was in those moments when the Military School, with its valiant young cadets, gave an example of what true devotion to duty meant; these young men knew that their school had already given various examples of the true meaning of honor, and they did not want to make a poor showing now. The cadets combatted in various places before arriving at Aljibes where their performance merited another brilliant page in history.

Carranza did not lose the hope of reaching Veracruz, but in order to accomplish this, he needed the support of the Chief of Operations of the State, General Guadalupe Sánchez, but the latter had also sworn allegiance to the Plan of Agua Prieta and this shattered the President's last hopes. In addition, the trains needed water, the machines having come to a halt due to the lack of this vital liquid. On May 13th Treviño's emissary arrived with the purpose of offering Carranza a plan for leaving the country, giving him guarantees to accomplish this. The President declined. General Francisco L. Urquizo, an eye-witness to these events, describes the incident in the following manner: "He was offered ample guarantees for his person. The message did not receive a reply. The President's face wreathed into a sardonic smile: 'Escape!' How very little General Treviño understood him. . . he who had been his direct commander for so long a time. . . No, the man who had confronted and defeated Victoriano Huerta, who had dominated Villa and overthrown him, who had stood erect and proudly in the face of American arrogance, who had sacrificed his own brother without hesitation, who had educated a breed of illustrious men, who had redeemed a nation could not flee in such a manner. 'I am not a coward, and I never have been."

In Aljibes —a small flag station— they decided to abandon the convoy. It was impossible to continue. The machines needed water and the troops were defecting. The civilians began to look for refuge in nearby ranches and small towns. Disorder prevailed, but above all was the might of the enemy. General Urquizo in his above-mentioned book affirms: "We were perfectly aware, from the President of the Republic on down to the last soldier, that we were lost, the road to Veracruz was blocked, we were friendless and cruelly vanquished by forces superior in number and morale. . ." In effect, on May 13th the situation became critical. Enemy attacks became more frequent. Another eye-witness, General Adolfo León Ossorio, describes the attack thus: "The windows of the railroad cars broke into pieces riddled by the bullets of the rebels. The civilians scattered, running for cover trying to find a place to protect themselves from the fusillade of shots. One woman, who carried in her busom a bundle full of jewelry, was stalked by the victorius soldiers who tore at her clothes, pushing her from one side to another with lustful hands. Ríos Zertuche unsheathed his sword and saved her by striking heavy blows and taking her to one of the cars. . ."

General Lucio Blanco, considered for many reasons which have been acknowledged, one of the most humane of the revolutionaries, was mounted on his horse during the most anguished moments at Aljibes. Realizing that no one would be able to alleviate the situation, and knowing that if he were taken prisoner there was no question but that he would be executed because Obregón had had it in for him for a long time now, exchanged some words with Osorio whom he profoundly admired, saying to him: "We've got to save the President!"

This was the chaotic situation endured in the tragic hours of the 13th; on the 14th, after a hasty meeting, it was decided to continue the march to the Puebla mountain range, where it was supposed loyal forces existed and thence continue northward. It was a hazardous undertaking, for the road was seemingly endless and uncertain. Most probably in Don Venustiano's deepest self he knew his end was near.

Let us return to the testimony of General Urquizo, who, in addition to being an eye-witness, was an excellent writer. In his book *The Assassination of Carranza,* he transcribes a conversation he had with the President:

"Sir, we are lost; there is no way out" —said Urquizo. "We have to escape. There is no doubt that the enemy will be here in a few minutes. Please leave."

"No." Carranza replied in complete control of himself, with the slow careful speech which was his wont, "General Murguía is going to organize the troops to withhold the advance. I am not leaving here."

"I am not leaving here."

"Sir," I implored, "leave before it's too late! Neither General Murguía nor anyone else can organize the troops now. Everyone is panicking; it's completely impossible."

"I'm not leaving here."

Nevertheless, the civilians were ordered to scatter and try to seek shelter as they could do little to help in such anguished circumstances.

Only the Military School remained loyal, playing a dramatic and glorious role, worthy of the best traditions of any army in the world. We shall transcribe the Squadron's Cavalry charge led by their Commander, Colonel Rodolfo

Casillas, which now forms part of the long history of honorable action of the Military School of Mexico.

In an article published in 1952 written by General Casillas and entitled "The Military School and Tlaxcalantongo" he describes the march of the cadets and their actions. Of these we shall describe only one of the charges of the students of the Cavalry School against the rebels.

"Apizaco could be likened to an anthill with so many military men, civilians and soldiers who had poured out of trains invading the town. Every place was jammed: the inns, the streets and particularly the stores and market places. The motley and noisy crowd gave no sign of the catastrophe about to occur, the tragic helter-skelter to come; few even realized the harsh and cruel certainty which already soared over our heads and which was to have its fatal denouement days later in Aljibes, the site of the tragedy."

In effect, the feasting, the gathering of provisions, the clamor of the troops and civilians of Carranza's government in Apizaco ceased upon the issuance of the order to embark. The train would be leaving at any moment as the men leading the charge approached the town, anxiously hoping to prove their worth in the eyes of their leader by attacking the Presidential convoy. Slowly, ever so slowly the trains wended their way towards San Marcos. By that time the Cavalry School and some mounted groups led by General Margarito Puente had already received precise orders to cover the rear guard of the trains. In the meantime, while the latter positioned themselves, we abandoned the railroad station's cluttered platforms congested with numerous railroad cars, and finally left the town which was saturated with people causing disturbances and blocking the way.

Anxious to breathe fresh cool air and gain access to a more limpid and clear atmosphere, and an open free field, the extensive limits of which would be lost in the distance, as well as to comply with the mission entrusted to us, we headed for a group of hills a short distance from the train, which due precisely to their proximity and quite favorable position afforded the convoy protection. The land was not what one could really consider unobstructed. It was made up of widely spread hills full of leaves on which had been planted hundreds of maguey plants, the aligned rows of which were lost in the distance, many kilometers away, merging with the lovely blue horizon. We had barely reached the highest point of the cluster of hills when we perceived the Obregón forces at a relatively short distance, composed of infantry and cavalry, advancing resolutely towards Apizaco.

"The proximity of the enemy no longer permitted us to take possession of the land or proceed to organize and defend ourselves by means of foot combat, which military tactics dictate when one is faced with lack of time. Nor was it prudent to use the horses and fire the carbines because these tactics in such a situation would result in nothing but a useless, fruitless waste of ammunition. Due to the above, and in consideration of the fact that on many occasions the best defense consists in an offense, the idea took shape in our leader's mind, instinctively and simply, to rapidly and decidedly organize as soon as circumstances so dictated, the saber charge consisting of various lines of purveyors against the enemy, which had continued its determined advance, the first volleys from which we began to receive."

"The saber charge against the enemy!"

"The ideals, illusions and longing of one's dreams or at the very least those dreams once entertained by the real dragoon."

"The epic charge of the cavalry, the heroic impetuous and lightning gallop in which the vertigo of speed and madness of fearless souls cleave wind and distance, flourishing the naked saber, man's weapon, held in trembling and fervent hands; a meteor-like advance in which one must be bold of heart, vibrant with ardor and courage, tempered by the moral strength of compliance with duty and spurred on by faith in worthy causes, as was the case in these particular circumstances. . . thus was the Military students' unswerving, non-evasive loyalty, devoid of subterfuge, to the laws and tenets of the Carranza regime."

"The cavalry charge: Here we see the glorious and impressive spectacle, the sublime ambitious gesture, the powerful magnet drawing the gallant cavalry cadets of the Military School who gave free rein to their courage and enthusiasm, when the High Command's decision began to crystallize and they heard the energetic, vibrant voice cry out: 'Take up your sabers!' This order was given by the no less brave section commanders of those unforgettable squadrons of brave young men. Then, at the command: 'Charge!' the young centurions hurled themselves like an uncontainable avalanche, a violent hurricane, something akin to a demon's curse on the host of Obregón followers commanded by General Máximo Rojas y Reyes Márquez on that memorable day in May 1920."

"The result was perforce logical and irrevocable. The denouement could be no other than that which had been anticipated: certain and inevitable. The result of the above charge, due to the material and moral forces it encompassed, was the forced and obligated retreat and the irremissible headlong flight of the enemy, overcome by fear and surprise."

"Nevertheless, we had advanced so rapidly that we were able to reach and even outdistance some of the flee- ing enemy so that a portion of our purveyors were mixed in with them, which resulted in veritable confusion. But our men reacted and without hesitation waged a furious battle with Reyes Márquez's men. Minutes later a group of our mounted companions joined the fray, led by General Pilar R. Sánchez who was able to shoot down some of the rebels with his .45."

"We did not continue in pursuit of the enemy for we did not want to move too far away from the trains as it was growing dark. Once the school was reorganized on its own territory, we returned to the railroad tracks continuing along the embankment in the direction of San Marcos, our goal for that day."

This concludes the description offered by General Ca- sillas, at that time Commander of the Cavalry School. Let us see the end of the cadets' action, penned by the oft- mentioned General Urquizo, in his book *México-Tlaxca- lantongo* in which he states:

"Near Santa María the Cavalry Squadron of the Mili- tary School came out to meet us. Colonel Casillas, respect- fully requested my orders."

'With your squadron please escort the President of the Republic' I told him, and the brilliant group of warriors and loyal young men joined the rear guard of our diminish- ing column of fugitives. . ."

"In correct military formation, the Cavalry Squadron of the Military School covered the rear guard, the only organized troops we had left. . ."

"After the recent defeat, the terrible debacle, everyone marched with the same indifference, the same courage, the same integrity with which fiery youth is endowed, almost as if they were entering the training camp of their Military School. In like manner, and with the same courage, they had left Mexico, and led by their worthy commander, sabers in hand, charged the enemy in Apizaco. Indeed it was almost as if they were confronted with a planned maneuver and not a bitter and bloody battle."

"In that very manner, with a smile on lips of budding moustaches, they had fought in Rinconada, at the rear guard of the convoys, resisting the violent thrust of the strong nucleus of enemy cavalry and had awaited with firm stance without firing a shot, undaunted, with unbelievable devotion, until the enemy was practically upon them and then they had annihilated it completely, wiping out its ranks and dispersing all survivors."

"In a similar manner they would now engage in battle. . . glorious and loyal cadets. . . worthy successors of the heroes of '47."

On the 18th Don Venustiano Carranza did not wish to continue sacrificing that noble and invigorated group of young men and ordered their return to Mexico. We shall continue Urquizo's commentary:

"As agreed upon with the President, at the first fork in the road we were travelling, the Military School Squadron would leave us. Their commander, Colonel Casillas, was so advised and Mr. Carranza's motives for making this decision explained to him, motives which more than making light of the small column had a profound moral origin in that all hope was lost: at any moment the enemy would overtake us; we would be overcome and captured. Was there any reason now to sacrifice that squadron of valiant men? What would be gained by it? Above all, with what right could this supreme sacrifice be demanded of those cadets who, when the critical moment arrived, would certainly fight and die in an unequal battle?"

"Why should they be obligated to do what the rest of the members of the Army hierarchy had not done? The latter were more obligated morally to comply with their duties, for in addition to their commitment as soldiers, they had a still greater obligation: their friends."

"...Casillas would not accept for any reason whatsoever the order which I had given him. His honor as a worthy soldier was offended, upon considering that he was being ordered to withdraw at the very moment when his services, and those of the troops at his command, were most useful. His duty was there, at the side of the lawful President. His obligations were precisely those of being useful, even if it meant the ultimate sacrifice. Occasions such as the above-described rarely arise wherein a soldier dies in the performance of his most sacred duty: loyalty. On the counter of a dilapidated country store, the only one in the place, I prepared the written order given to the Squadron of the Military School to abandon us. In the reglamentary ceremonial phrases I injected the sincere emotion which overcame me. Casillas received the order and was deeply moved; he was choked with emotion. The cadets awaited; their youthful countenances reflected their bitterness in leaving us. Down deep in their young hearts they experienced the intense emotion of abandoning the path we had traced for them at their school. In their loyal breasts they were proud to protect the weak, and in that situation we were the weak, and their duties as soldiers were pledged to us. They were overcome with the profound wish for sacrifice and the obscure phantoms of their glorious predecessers who had died in Chapultepec illuminated their fantasies. . ."

Thus was the history of the Military School written on that dramatic and glorious day. The Squadron made a half turn and marched to Mexico City, covered with legitimate glory, while President Carranza, who represented legality, entered the cold and cloudy hills of Puebla. Both had complied with their duties. History woud give the final verdict.

That small group which represented outraged dignity entered those misty mountains, crossing small towns with Indian names made up of small groups of hovels indiscriminately crowded together. Groups of ignorant people came out to watch the horsemen, who fatigued, continued their onerous trip. They travelled through San Francisco Ixtamamtitlan, Tecahuitl, Zitlacuatla, Tetela de Ocampo, names which do not even appear on geographical maps; miserable hamlets inhabited by even more miserable people. The penultimate town: Patla; there "the people of Herrero" approached them, thus known because they served General Rodolfo Herrero, who a short time later appeared before Carranza, making him promises of loyalty and allegiance to his person and regime. The march continued; at 5:00 p.m. they arrived at a town more miserable than all the others: San Antonio Tlaxcalantongo. It was not really a town, just a tiny conglomeration of adobe huts.

Everyone arrived exhausted, physically and morally defeated, not knowing whether the forces surrounding them, or those awaiting them, were loyal or had become supporters of the Agua Prieta Plan. The President ordered that they should stay the night there. The party distributed themselves in the poor hovels of the place. Food was poor and scarce. The hut chosen by Carranza had a surface area of four by five meters; it had a dirt floor, there was no light or electricity, only the door and a small window which afforded a bit of light in the somber night. In the hut he was accompanied by Attorney Aguirre Berlanga, Secretary of the Interior, Mario Méndez, Pedro Gil Farías, his private secretary and his aides-de-camp, Captains Octavio Amador and Ignacio Suárez as well as his adjutant, Secundino Reyes.

Once more we return to General Urquizo for the story of Carranza's last hours. From his book *The Asassination of Carranza,* we extract the following dialogue:

"I don't think we're doing too well" —said Urquizo.

"Why, General?"

"Because we have absolutely no fodder for the horses; not having any food for ourselves is the least of it but the horses are tired and hungry."

"That's true, we're not too well off here and we could travel some four or five leagues more; it's still early, but we have to wait for news from Mariel to find out how the road up ahead is."

From another eye-witness to these dramatic hours, Lieut. Colonel Suárez, we have extracted the following paragraph:

"What was happening in the environs of Tlaxcalantongo? We already know that in the northern part of the Puebla hills, occupied by the forces of Colonel Gabriel Barrios, who had pledged his allegiance to the Agua Prieta Plan, the column was allowed to continue without encountering any hostility but neither did the Colonel offer any help. He confined himself to informing us in an offhand manner that cavalry troops led by General Guajardo were in Tetela in pursuit of the loyal column. This covered the southeast. South of Villa Juárez in Huauchinango, enemy forces commanded by General Jesús Novoa were stationed. In the northeast it was well known that General Arnulfo R. Gómez, Chief of Operations in Northern Veracruz, had joined the rebellion and with him were the leaders of the groups commanded by him. One of these groups was stationed in the south of Papantla at a point known as Espinal for the purpose of attacking the loyal column. . ."

Now let us return to Don Venustiano's remaining hours, as described by his aide-de-camp, Lieut. Colonel Ignacio Suárez, who wrote:

"A little before dawn at 4:00 a.m., without a single noise to announce the presence of strangers near the Indian hut, a volley of rifle shots sounded close by to the rear of the hut, accompanied by stentorian cries of 'Long Live Obregón', 'Long Live Peláez', 'Down with Carranza' and insults of the worst kind. Captains Suárez and Amador stood up immediately and ran out of the lodgings and did not notice anyone approach the door or any noise whatsoever on that side.

Immediately after firing their arms, the attackers withdrew and silence again reigned. Moments later a new volley of shots was heard but now far from the Indian hut. Suárez returned to the interior of the hut to help the President out because, if the attack were to be repeated, no defense could be made from the inside due to the flimsiness of the walls.

"Attorney Aguirre Berlanga who was resting about a meter and a half from Mr. Carranza's bed has stated that immediately after the volley of shots, the President groaned for he had been wounded, and said: 'Attorney Aguirre, I see green.'

"When Suárez reached the President's side unable to hurry due to the darkness which prevailed, and taking his bearings from the table located in the center of the room, he came close to Carranza and said: 'Sir, Sir.'

"He was about to state his purpose of helping him to leave when he heard the death rattle which revealed the President's moribund state. . . Suárez realized the President had expired, and gently lowered him to the bed. He stood up and looking at his luminous watch, announced:

'The President has just expired. Take note: it is 4:20 a.m.'

Thus ended the life of Venustiano Carranza, victim of the political strife which had caused Mexico so much damage.

The rest of his companions were captured; some managed to escape at different points in the hills.

Much has been written about this political crime. Rodolfo Herrero, who was the actual perpetrator of the crime, because it was his forces who executed the attack, never cleared up the part he played in spite of the fact that he survived the terrible event for many years.

Nevertheless, immediately rumors that Carranza had committed suicide abounded, a story spread by Herrero's followers and by the General himself, who perhaps was overcome by the tremendous historical responsibility of his act.

The body was transferred to Mexico City by a group of his followers. Among them were Ignacio L. Bonillas, the engineer who had been the indirect cause of the tragedy and who later abandoned politics forever, retiring to the United States. Also accompanying the remains were General Francisco Murguía, General Urquizo, General Juan Barragán, Attorney Aguirre Berlanga, and others. Mr. Carranza was buried in Dolores Cemetary. On the preceding day, the Congress of the Union had designated Mr. Adolfo de la Huerta —one of the leaders of the Agua Prieta movement— as substitute President of the Republic.

Carranza's companions upon arriving in Mexico City, were put on trial, while Herrero remained free. At the end of 1920 he was put on trial for the crimes of violence against the people in general as well as homicide at the Second Military Instruction Court of the city, which was in charge of conducting the trial.

The second judge of Military Instruction granted Herrero conditional freedom. Nevertheless on January 1, 1921, by Presidential Decree, General Enrique Estrada ordered General Rodolfo Herrero's dismissal from the army as he was considered unworthy of that institution. A few years later Herrero returned to active service during the rebel uprisings of de la Huerta's supporters and during Escobar's rebellion in 1929. However, in 1938, when General Lázaro Cárdenas was President of the Republic, Herrero was again dismissed from the army, this time definitively. Herrero established his residence in Monterrey, where he lived for many years and with him died important secrets regarding this national tragedy, which were never cleared up.

The election of de la Huerta initiated the long era of government by Sonora politicians. Among them were Adolfo de la Huerta, General Alvaro Obregón and General Plutarco Elías Calles who were to govern the country until 1928, in spite of the fact that General Calles wielded considerable political influence until General Cárdenas, upon becoming President, decided to expel him from the country.

Mr. de la Huerta formed his cabinet with the following people: Secretary of the Interior, Attorney Gilberto Valenzuela; Secretary of War, General Plutarco Elías Calles;

Secretary of the Treasury, General Salvador Alvarado; Industry and Commerce, General Jacinto B. Treviño; Communications and Public Works, Engineer and General Pascual Ortiz Rubio; Foreign Affairs, Miguel Covarrubias; Agriculture and Development of Industries, General Antonio I. Villarreal. The distinguished José Vasconcelos was designated Rector of the National University.

De la Huerta's term in office lasted until November 30, 1920. His government was in general a good one as personally he was an honest, simple and austere man who disliked pomp, and, in addition, he realized that Mexico was prostrate after long civil strife and that everyone's collaboration was necessary to put the country back on its feet.

One of the most important acts of his governmental term was the appeasement of Villa who for several years marauded about the northern part of the country and was a latent menace.

The first attempts were made through General Ignacio C. Enríquez, Governor of Chihuahua, but were unsuccessful.

Before surrendering, Villa attacked a few towns in Chihuahua, among them the capital city. The old guerrilla had merited the profound hatred of Obregón and Calles, and the latter did not wish to make any pacts with him. Nevertheless, Villa was able to sustain telegraphic communication with the new President and de la Huerta, who sought conciliation and accepted Villa's terms, which consisted of being granted a hacienda and an escort of his old followers (dorados). Obregón, who was campaigning, was opposed to these arrangements; he sent a telegram to the governors and Military Operations Chiefs in which he expressed himself as follows:

*"General Villa has attacked the american city of Columbus, where he committed acts of misbehavior and violence. It is only natural that when the American Embassy becomes aware that we are giving him support, they will request the extradition of the impulsive guerrilla from Durango. Then what can we do?"*

Nevertheless, in spite of General Obregón's objections, it was ordered that the negotiations continue. General Eugenio Martínez, Chief of Operations at La Laguna, was commissioned for this purpose. Martínez was finally able to interview Villa at Sabinas. There, after discussions and negotiations, a pact was signed on July 28, 1920, in which it was decided that Villa was to withdraw to the Hacienda of Canutillo, Durango, where he could maintain an escort of 500 men chosen by him and paid for by the Ministry of War and Navy.

Both parties accepted, and Villa retired to this hacienda where he would live only three years, as he was assassinated in 1923, and thus ended his unfortunate life.

Another famous surrender was that of General Félix Díaz who from 1913 had risen in rebellion, and, as we may remember, had been one of the principal enemies of Madero's government and who had played a prominent part in the events of the Tragic Ten Days.

De la Huerta gave orders so that Félix Díaz, who had given himself up voluntarily to the new government and had declared that his life as a revolutionary had terminated, be allowed to leave the country, offering him $ 10,000.00

dollars, which were dollars. This offer was turned down by ex-General Díaz who left the country to live in exile.

Another famous personage, although of less importance, was General Jesús Guajardo who had prepared the ambush which caused the death of Emiliano Zapata. This man, now a general, rose in rebellion in 1920 against de la Huerta. His movement was unsuccessful and he failed peremptorily. He was captured in Monterrey, put on trial and shot on July 17th of that year.

Also General Pablo González, who had played a prominent role in the Revolution, although he had not had much luck, but had been a protégé of Carranza, although he had abandoned at the last moment, was part of an attempted rebellion against the new government. He was captured in the city of Monterrey, tried and condemned to death, but thanks to the intervention of Attorney Miguel Alessio Robles, he was able to obtain de la Huerta's pardon. To this end, a short time later a telegram was sent to General Manuel Pérez Treviño, Chief of Military Operations at Nuevo León, ordering the immediate release of the prisoner.

In addition, a few generals who had supported Zapata, upon perceiving the magnanimity of the new Chief of State, made overtures to the government to surrender and keep the peace. Among them was General Genovevo de la O.

The same thing occurred with General Alberto Pineda who maintained a rebellious attitude in the faraway State of Chiapas; negotiations were carried out and finally this general changed his attitude, bringing peace to that part of the Republic.

But peace was not sought only in the distant south; it was also sought in the peninsula of Lower California where for some years Colonel Esteban Cantú had governed in a quasi-independent position; here de la Huerta's government displayed great activity and finally managed to obtain peaceful surrender of the government; Colonel Cantú went to Los Angeles and General Abelardo Rodríguez was put in charge of the Northern Territory of Lower California.

It was necessary to resolve the sitation of some of the Governments of the Federation which had not joined the Plan of Agua Prieta, for which reason the Senate designated provisional governors for the States of Campeche, Guanajuato, Jalisco, México, Puebla, Querétaro, Tamaulipas and Yucatán.

In September de la Huerta delivered his Report before Congress, in which he stated: "All of the goals have not been accomplished, due to the shortness of time which your present Head of Executive Powers has at his command (only three months) to fulfill his duties, due to other basic reasons which you are aware of, although he is in a position to confirm that he has been successful in channeling efforts for the solution of some of these problems." Further on he declared that: "Carranza having been defeated by the force of public opinion which was manifested all over the country by the allegiance of all the States to the aforementioned Plan, the Supreme Head of this liberating movement issued a summons to the General Congress for the election of a Substitute President of the United Mexican States. . ."

Among other important accomplishments during his term of office was the appeasement of the bellicose Yaqui tribe which inhabited the southern part of the State of Sonora.

At the end of that year, presidential elections were held, and as was absolutely logical, General Alvaro Obregón was elected.

On December 1, 1920, the Sonora leader took his oath of office. The country anticipated a new era of peace and prosperity, which unfortunately was still not to be.

The Obregón Cabinet was composed of the following: Foreign Affairs, Doctor Cutberto Hidalgo; Ministry of the Interior, General Plutarco Elías Calles; Treasury Department, ex-President Adolfo de la Huerta; War and Navy Department, General Benjamín Hill; Agriculture and Development of Industries, General Antonio I. Villarreal; Industry, Commerce and Labor, Attorney Rafael Zubaran Campmany; Public Works, General and Engineer Pascual Ortiz Rubio.

With Obregón a new stage in the life of Mexico was initiated: that which is known as the Revolutionary Governments. During this decade Mexico would still undergo various revolutionary movements, which did not have the magnitude or importance of the ones we have seen previously. As of 1930, the country entered a period of stability, which with the exception of the small uprising of Cedillo in 1938, has continued with no interruptions of consequence.

The Mexican Revolution was a great social movement which, like all events of this nature, caused much suffering and bloodshed, but the end result was the birth of a new country which now strives to march towards its destiny along the paths of peace and prosperity.

# BIBLIOGRAPHY

RICCIUS FRANCESCO. *La Revolución Mexicana*. Ed. Bruguera. 1976.

SILVA HERZOG, JESUS. *Breve Historia de la Revolución Mexicana*. 2 Volúmenes. Fondo de Cultura Económica. 1960.

MARQUEZ STERLING, MANUEL. *Los Días Finales del Presidente Madero*. Ed. Porrúa, S.A. 1958.

REYES, RODOLFO. *De mi Vida. Memorias Políticas*. Volúmenes I y II. Librería Madrid. 1929.

CASASOLA, ARCHIVOS. *Historia Gráfica de la Revolución*. Segunda Ed. Crónica Ilustrada de la Revolución Mexicana. Ed. Publex. 1966.

SANCHEZ LAMEGO, M.A. General. *Historia Militar de la Revolución Constitucionalista*.

COTA GUILLERMO. CAPT. *Historia Militar de México*. Ensayo, México 1947.

ALESSIO ROBLES, MIGUEL. *Historia Política de la Revolución* Mexicana. Ed. Botas, México 1946.

TABLADA, JOSE JUAN. *Historia de la Campaña de la División del Norte*. Ed. 1913.

DULLES W.F., JOHN. *Ayer en México*. F.C.E. 1977.

GUZMAN ESPARZA, ROBERTO. *Memorias de Adolfo de la Huerta*. México 1957.

MARQUEZ B., MIGUEL. *El Real Tlaxcalantongo*. México 1941.

URQUIZO, FRANCISCO. Gral. *Historia del Ejército y la Revolución Constitucionalista*. México.

TARACENA, ALFONSO. *Venustiano Carranza*. Ed. Jus.

CAMPOS, ARMANDO DE MARIA. *Vida del General Lucio Blanco*. Instituto de Estudios sobre la Revolución Mexicana.

LICEAGA, LUIS. *General Félix Díaz*. Ed. Jus. 1958.

CAMPOS, ARMANDO DE MARIA. *Múgica: Biografía*. México.

TUCHMAN, BARBARA. *El Telegrama Zimmermann*. Ed. Grijalbo. 1960.

Other titles in the **PANORAMA** series

# HISTORY

# ARCHAEOLOGY AND ANTHROPOLOGY

# ART

# POPULAR ART

Other titles in the **PANORAMA** series

## TRADITIONS

### MEN AND HORSES OF MEXICO
*José Alvarez del Villar*

## TITLES BEING PREPARED

### INDIAN COSTUMES OF MEXICO
*Ruth D. Lechuga*

### THE MEXICAN HIGH TEMPLE
*Elizabeth Baquedano*

Printed in:
Impresora Múltiple, S.A. de C.V.
Bolivia No. 55 Local 11
Col. Centro
06020 México, D.F.
1000 Copies
Mexico City, June, 1990